Decorative Arts
Highlights

Decorative Arts Highlights

from the
Wendy and Emery Reves
Collection

Charles L. Venable

with frame entries by Richard R. Brettell
Barbara Scott, Research Assistant
Tom Jenkins, Photographer

DALLAS MUSEUM OF ART

This handbook was made possible by the Dallas Museum of Art League.

Edited by Queta Moore Watson, with assistance from Patricia Draher
Designed by John Hubbard

Produced by Marquand Books, Inc., Seattle

Printed and bound by C & C Offset Printing, Hong Kong

Library of Congress Cataloging-in-Publication Data
Dallas Museum of Art.
    Decorative arts highlights from the Wendy and Emery Reves collection / Charles L. Venable with frame entries by Richard R. Brettell ; Barbara Scott, research assistant ; Tom Jenkins, photographer.
        p.   cm.
    ISBN 0-936227-16-8 (paper : alk. paper). —
    ISBN 0-936227-17-6 (set : alk. paper)
        1. Decorative arts—Europe—Catalogs. 2. Decorative arts—Asia—Catalogs. 3. Reves, Emery, 1904–1981—Art collections—Catalogs. 4. Reves, Wendy, 1916-   —Art collections—Catalogs. 5. Decorative arts—Texas—Dallas—Catalogs. 6. Dallas Museum of Art—Catalogs. I. Venable, Charles L. (Charles Lane), 1960-   . II. Title.
NK925.D35   1995
745'.074'7642812—dc20   95-23921

Frontispiece: Chinese porcelain wall fountain (detail), p. 97.

Contents

for Wendy Reves

Foreword

Wendy Reves entered the life of the Dallas Museum of Art at a most propitious moment. Under the directorship of Harry Parker, the Dallas Museum of Art had already set its sights on enriching the artistic life of this vigorous and ambitious city. Plans were well underway for the move from Fair Park into stylish new facilities downtown. The moment could not have been more appropriate for the meeting of patron and museum director that was to be of such immense importance to this community. The bond that formed between these two remarkable people, Wendy Reves and Harry Parker, culminated in the astonishing gift to the DMA that is chronicled in this volume and its companion volume on the fine arts. It is now ten years since the Reves galleries first opened and the fortunes of this museum took a decided turn. Therefore, with profound gratitude, we celebrate that signal event with two handsome publications and the accompanying exhibition of the most significant and stellar objects in the Wendy and Emery Reves Collection.

Thanks are due to Charles L. Venable, Chief Curator and Curator of Decorative Arts, who served as project organizer and principal author of the decorative arts catalogue, and to Richard R. Brettell, who succeeded Harry Parker as director in Dallas, for his authorship of the volume on fine arts. The timely and generous financial assistance of the Dallas Museum of Art League was essential to the successful completion of this noteworthy project.

Ultimately, however, it is to Wendy Reves that this effort must be dedicated. We cannot but admire the extraordinary generosity that moved her to empty her beloved Villa La Pausa of its contents so as to enrich the citizens of Dallas. Her name must join the ranks of those distinguished museum patrons who have changed the course of institutions and forever nourished the lives of countless museum visitors.

Jay Gates
Director
Dallas Museum of Art

Preface and Acknowledgments

The gift of the Wendy and Emery Reves Collection profoundly changed the Dallas Museum of Art. Obviously, the addition of numerous fine impressionist paintings, works on paper, and sculptures greatly enhanced the Museum's holdings. However, the impact of the Reves decorative arts was more profound.

Before the early 1980s, the DMA did not collect in the area of European and American decorative arts. The arrival of the Reves Collection was a catalyst for change. With the acceptance of the collection, the DMA instantly acquired over 1,000 examples of European and Asian applied arts. Suddenly, the Museum had significant holdings in the areas of rugs, glass, metalwork, porcelain, furniture, and frames. This is a handbook of the finest objects in each of these categories.

The impact of the Reves gift went well beyond the mere presence of decorative arts objects in the DMA. Very shortly after Wendy Reves decided to donate her extraordinary collection, local decorative arts enthusiasts approached the Museum with ideas of how to build on this new foundation. For example, they suggested acquisitions be made in the American decorative arts to balance the new European holdings. By the opening of the Reves galleries in 1985, enough support had been gathered to purchase an important collection of 18th- and early 19th-century American furniture. The next year, I arrived as the DMA's first curator of decorative arts. In 1987, a support group called Friends of Decorative Arts was founded.

Since the magnanimous gift of the Reves Collection, Dallas's decorative arts department has grown rapidly. Besides American furniture, especially noteworthy acquisitions include 18th-century British silver and 19th- and early 20th-century American silver. The latter collection grew to such strength that it became the centerpiece for the first traveling decorative arts exhibition ever organized by Dallas, *Silver in America, 1840–1940: A Century of Splendor* (1994). Similar growth in the field of 20th-century design has laid the foundation for the upcoming exhibition *Hot Cars, High Fashion, Cool Stuff: Designs of the 20th Century* (1996).

Though I have found Dallas to be an energetic and often amazing city, I have no doubt that the accomplishments of the past decade in the area of decorative arts would not have occurred without Wendy Reves's amazing gift. However, the presence of Reves in this city has been as important as her donations. As one who has had the good fortune of knowing Wendy Reves better than most, I can attest to the fact that she is indeed a rare person whose generosity and caring spirit is equaled by few others. Without her, Dallas and its art museum would without question be less exciting. Both personally and on behalf of my fellow Dallasites, I want to thank Wendy Reves for all she has done for this great city.

Although this book would not have been possible without the help and encouragement of Wendy Reves, who collected most of the objects illustrated on its pages, many of my professional colleagues have also been most helpful and generous with their knowledge. Richard Brettell's keen insight into the frames in the Reves Collection and his authorship of the entries on those selected for publication were a great help. Also of value were the opinions of Gillian Wilson, Dwight Lanmon, Clare Le Corbeillier, Donald Fennimore, Michael Gregory, Anna Bennett, David Owsley, Charles Avery, Anthony du Boulay, Th. H. Scheurleer, Barbara Roberts, David Johnson, and John P. Smith. Of those on staff at the DMA, special mention should go to Ron Moody, Debra Wittrup, Queta Moore Watson, and Tom Jenkins. But it is Barbara Scott who as a volunteer has gone far beyond the call of duty in her efforts to research numerous pieces in the collection. Without her efforts, this project would have been much more difficult. Finally, I wish to thank the Dallas Museum of Art League, whose financial commitment made possible the publication of this volume and its companion.

Dr. Charles L. Venable
Chief Curator and Curator of Decorative Arts
Dallas Museum of Art

Metalwork

During the 1960s and 1970s, Wendy and Emery Reves amassed more than 200 pieces of ironwork ranging in date from the 15th to the 19th century. Much of this collection was acquired from a dealer in Salzburg, Austria. Occasionally, the couple purchased important single pieces from other dealers. The Roman lockplate, for example, was bought in 1967 from French & Company in New York. Exceptional items like the lockplate were displayed on velvet-covered bases as sculpture at the couple's home on the French Riviera, Villa La Pausa. Other pieces, many of which were restored by the Reveses' staff, were used to create decorative patterns on the white stucco interior walls of the villa.

The silver in the collection is almost all English and with few exceptions was purchased in London between 1962 and 1964 for use by the Reveses. The set of four Le Sage candelabra came from Thomas Lumley, while the octagonal casters were acquired from N. Bloom & Sons. Mrs. G. E. P. How of London not only sold the couple the Le Sage tray but supplied the gilt dessert flatware as well. She also assembled for her clients eighteen place settings of early 18th-century flatware, which are now divided between Villa La Pausa and the Dallas Museum of Art. The pair of candlesticks by Bache was given to Wendy and Emery Reves by Mary Lasker as a wedding present in 1964. Lasker had purchased them in London from Spink & Son.

LOCKPLATE

Probably Germany, c. 1475–1525
Iron
H. 13¾ in. (34.9 cm), w. 17¾ in. (45.1 cm)
1985.R.797

ALONG WITH MASONRY architecture and stained glass, one of the most developed of the applied arts in medieval Europe was wrought iron. The metal had long been used for functional purposes, but during the Middle Ages blacksmiths in central Europe raised the forging and ornamenting of iron to a level unseen since antiquity.

Originally part of the fittings for a large wooden door, this lockplate is an exceptional example of Germanic metalworking during the late Gothic period. Although lockplates with scalloped edges and applied tracery were made in many European cities, the delicacy of the iron appliqués on this piece and the decorative terminals on the scallops' points suggest a great German metalworking center like Nuremberg.

BOX

France, c. 1475–1550
Wood and iron
H. 4½ in. (11.4 cm), W. 6½ in. (16.5 cm),
D. 4¾ in. (12.1 cm)
1985.R.816

SMALL PORTABLE BOXES like this one are believed to have been used for transporting messages in the late medieval and early Renaissance periods. Constructed of a wooden core covered with sheets of wrought and pierced iron and fitted with a large lock, this box was well protected from the dangers inherent in travel during this era. The rings on the side were probably used to attach the box to the messenger's belt for further security.

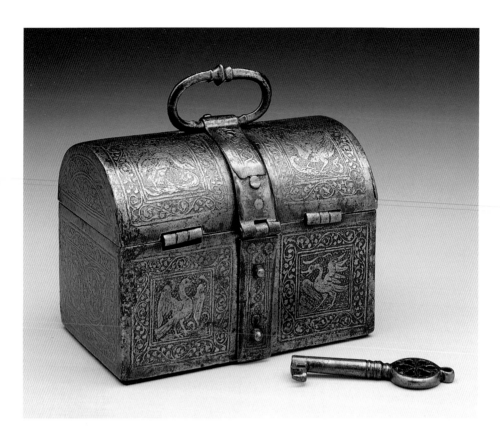

BOX
Probably Nuremberg, Germany, c. 1600–1700
Iron
H. 3½ in. (8.9 cm), w. 4¾ in. (12.1 cm),
D. 3⅛ in. (7.9 cm)
1985.R.815.a–b

MINIATURE STRONGBOXES like this example were popular among Europe's wealthy. Because they were made of iron, yet were relatively lightweight and featured a carrying ring, they provided a safe repository for coins, documents, and jewels that could be taken on journeys. This example has the added security feature of being two-faced. One side has the true hasp, the other a false one. Prying hands had to determine which hasp actually covered the keyhole before the lock could successfully be breached.

This box is decorated with birds and foliate scrollwork in square reserves. The desired ornament was "masked off" with varnish, and acid was applied to eat away the background. The south German city of Nuremberg was known for this type of etched decoration.

LOCKPLATE AND HASP
Probably Rome, Italy, c. 1550–1580
Gilt bronze and iron
H. 8⅞ in. (22.5 cm), W. 6⅞ in. (17.5 cm)
1985.R.814

AS CHARLES AVERY has pointed out, this superb lockplate was intended for use on a type of domed marriage chest *(cassone)* popular in late 16th-century Italy (Avery 1989). At present, there are over forty examples of this casting known in collections around the world, but the exact origin of this group has eluded scholars for decades. The French Fontainebleau School has been suggested because of the mannerist style of the figure of Abundance on the hasp. The trophies of arms, which were popular on Milanese and Genoese palace architecture, have directed others to these cities as possible places of manufacture. Nevertheless, the fact that the majority of the identifiable coats of arms are those of Roman families indicates that this lockplate design was most likely executed in Rome. Avery further notes that the mingling of numerous stylistic sources in this piece also suggests a Roman origin since the Eternal City was a confluence of international styles in the 16th century.

This example survives with its iron locking mechanism on the back. The coat of arms is believed to be that of the Gras-Préville family of Italy and southern France.

DOOR KNOCKER
France, c. 1700–1750
Iron
H. 15 in. (38.1 cm), W. 12½ in. (31.8 cm)
1985.R.806

MADE OF POLISHED IRON, this beautiful door knocker is a fine example of French 18th-century metalworking. The knocker itself is of wrought iron that was shaped on an anvil with hammers; the backplate was cut from sheet iron. The elaborate baroque-style scrollwork of the backplate is characteristic of early 18th-century examples, as is the use of decorative "buttons" where the knocker joins the hinge. A bolt behind the hinge secured the knocker to the door, while the backplate was held in place by nails driven through the visible holes.

TANKARD
Carsten Lauridsen, Copenhagen, Denmark,
1728
Silver
H. 8⅜ in. (21.3 cm), w. 8 in. (20.3 cm),
D. 6⅝ in. (16.8 cm)
1985.R.569

THIS TANKARD IS OF A FORM that was made in Denmark for at least a century beginning in the 1660s. The conical body, low domed cover, and scrolled handle seen here are all characteristic of this type. The use of lions holding balls for the feet and thumb piece was one of several options available. Other Danish examples are known that use pomegranates for these elements. The Reves tankard is especially noteworthy for its incorporation of coins. The practice of embedding coins and medals in silverwork was most popular in Baltic countries. Here, the sides are inset with three horizontal rows of kroner, minted between 1693 and 1696, that carry the profile of King Christian V wearing the Order of the Elephant. The lid encases a large medal of the king facing Queen Charlotte Amalie. The reverse of the medal appears on the underside of the lid and depicts the heads of five royal children. The medal was designed by Anton Meybusch and was cast in 1695 to celebrate the king's birthday on 15 April.

PAIR OF CANDLESTICKS
John Bache (w. 1673–1729), London, England,
1702
Britannia standard silver
H. 8½ in. (21.6 cm), DIAM. 4⅞ in. (12.4 cm)
1985.R.544–545

CANDLESTICKS OF THIS form were
popular in England around 1700. Highly
architectural in nature, each stick takes
the form of a stop-fluted Doric column.
The maker added mass to the design by
placing the column on a series of octagonal and round bases with gadrooned
edges. In keeping with much silverwork
made in London in this period, the metal
is worked very thinly. The raised decoration was created through repoussé
chasing, in which the metal is pushed
up from the reverse side.

The bottom rim of each stick is engraved with the initials *I P* under *P*. The
engraving that once decorated the shield-
shaped reserves on the bases has been
removed.

KNIFE, SPOON, AND FORK
(ONE OF EIGHTEEN PLACE SETTINGS)

Isaac Davenport (w. 1689–1731), London, England, 1706
Gilt silver
H. (knife) ¾ in. (1.9 cm), W. ¾ in. (1.9 cm), L. 7⅝ in. (19.4 cm);
H. (spoon) ¾ in. (1.9 cm), W. 1½ in. (3.8 cm), L. 7 in. (17.8 cm);
H. (fork) ½ in. (1.3 cm), W. ⅞ in. (2.2 cm), L. 6⅞ in. (17.5 cm)
1985.R.554.1, 553.1, 567.1

THIS TYPE OF spoon and fork is known to collectors today as "dog nose." The pattern first appeared in the late 1690s but was primarily produced between 1700 and 1715. Knives with beads at the tip of their handle were often made to accompany dog-nose-style flatware. The fact that the Reves examples survive as part of a service for eighteen makes them highly unusual. Also rare is the presence of four-tined forks in this pattern, as well as the use of gilding. The crest is that of the Earl of Cardigan. The service was probably given to George, the third Earl of Cardigan, for his wedding. In 1707, he married Elizabeth, the eldest daughter of Thomas Bruce, third Earl of Elgin and second Earl of Ailesbury.

The knives are unmarked.

PLATE (ONE OF TWELVE)
John Leach (w. 1682–1710), London, England,
1708
Britannia standard silver
H. ⅞ in. (2.2 cm), DIAM. 9⅞ in. (25.1 cm)
1985.R.547.1

FOLLOWING THE RETURN of Charles II
to the throne in 1660, much English
silver became highly elaborate under
the influence of foreign silversmiths who
accompanied the king back from the
continent, where he had been in exile. In
the early 18th century, a backlash against
this ornate baroque style affected English
silver. This plate, decorated only with a
coat of arms, is characteristic of those
made in the first decade of the new century. The Reves example is particularly
noteworthy because it survives as part of
a set of twelve, which is rare. The set,
which was broken up in 1920, originally
contained at least twenty plates. The
arms are those of Sir William Turner,
who became Lord Mayor of London
in 1669.

SET OF CASTERS

Thomas Tearle (w. 1707–1742), London, England, 1719
Britannia standard silver
H. (larger) 6½ in. (16.5 cm), DIAM. 2¾ in. (7 cm);
H. (smaller) 5¾ in. (14.6 cm), DIAM. 2⅜ in. (6 cm)
1985.R.549–551

FROM THE 16TH THROUGH the early 19th century, caster sets were necessary parts of a table service. Large ones, as in the center here, were probably used for dispensing sugar, and the smaller ones held imported spices like pepper. Salt was typically served in open trenchers. Casters were important forms in European silver until the late 19th century, when commodities like spices and sugar became commonplace and Westerners began switching to salt and pepper shakers.

This set is a fine example of early 18th-century English silver. Octagonal shapes that were constructed by soldering together panels of sheet silver were especially popular in this period. The decoration on these examples was achieved by piercing the tops with a drill and a jeweler's saw and by engraving the bodies with a sharp tool that cut tiny lines into the surface. Although the husband's coat of arms, incorporated into the left side of the engraving, is unidentified, the wife's is that of the Payne family of Petworth, Sussex.

FOOTED SALVER

John Hugh Le Sage (w. 1708–c. 1750s),
London, England, 1747
Sterling silver
H. 2⅛ in. (5.4 cm), w. 23⅝ in. (60 cm),
D. 18 in. (45.7 cm)
1985.R.546

JOHN LE SAGE WAS ONE of 18th-century England's finest silversmiths. Le Sage was apprenticed to Lewis Cuney in 1708 and became a free journeyman in 1718. Made late in his career, this salver reflects the fineness of much of Le Sage's work. It is in the new rococo taste that was popular at mid-century. Derived from Italian 17th-century decoration, the style matured in France during the 1730s and was brought to England by Huguenot silversmiths who were forced to flee France following the revocation of the Edict of Nantes in 1685, which had allowed the practice of Protestantism. Le Sage was of Huguenot descent.

Although the cast borders and paw feet are very fine, this salver is most noteworthy for its engraved decoration. Surrounding a coat of arms, likely that of the Farquharson family, are implements of war including cannon, bayonets, flags, drums, pikes, guns, powder kegs, and cannonballs. The crenellated tower and the monogram of King George II suggest that this tray was presented for distinguished service in battle, but no concrete evidence has yet been found to support this theory.

PAIR OF CANDELABRA (TWO OF FOUR)
John Hugh Le Sage (w. 1708–c. 1750s), London,
England, 1747
Augustus Le Sage (w. 1752–1790s), London,
England, 1771 (branches)
Sterling silver
H. 16½ in. (41.9 cm), w. 14½ in. (36.8 cm),
D. 5¾ in. (14.6 cm)
1985.R.540–541.a–b

THESE CANDELABRA were originally
made as candlesticks. They were converted into candelabra through the addition of two-arm branches in 1771. Such
additions were common because they
not only made the silver more impressive
in terms of scale, but increased the number of candles and hence the amount of
light. The branches on these examples
were executed by Augustus Le Sage,
the son of John Le Sage, who made the
candlesticks, and are in keeping with the
original rococo decoration. The bases of

the sticks have asymmetrical scrolled
borders, while the shafts feature shells
and pendant motifs.

These candelabra are engraved with
the crest of Sackville, Duke of Dorset.
Before leaving the family in 1962, they
were part of the furnishings of a well-
known countryseat called Drayton
House in Northamptonshire. Although
the structure primarily dates from the
16th and 17th centuries, parts of the
complex are from the 14th century.

Rugs and Fans

Wendy and Emery Reves's interest in textiles was wide ranging. Their collection contains examples of European silk fabrics and velvets, embroideries, lace, vestments, and bed coverings. However, their most distinguished accomplishments were in the area of rugs and fans.

In total, the Reveses assembled a fine group of approximately thirty rugs during the 1960s and 1970s. The collection remains mostly intact, with twenty-four examples in the Dallas Museum of Art. Three Spanish rugs and one Portuguese rug are still at Villa La Pausa but will be added to Dallas's holdings in the future.

Unlike most of their contemporaries, the Reveses were not particularly interested in rugs from Asia Minor. Rather, they built a collection that illustrates the history of rug weaving in southern Europe, especially Spain. To document the influence of specific types of Asian rugs on European design, the couple also collected a small number of pieces from Egypt, Turkey, and India. To procure exceptional examples, they worked closely with the well-known Parisian firm of Tarica, Ltd. Furthermore, Emery Reves corresponded widely with numerous specialists in the field, including Ulrich Schürmann, L. Bernheimer, Kurt Erdmann, Friedrich Spuhler, Angela Volker, and Charles Grant Ellis.

The fan collection was of particular interest to Wendy Reves. Today, her collection numbers approximately 110 examples, of which 38 are now in Dallas. She collected examples dating from the early 18th to the early 20th century; those at the Dallas Museum of Art represent the core of her 18th-century holdings.

"HOLBEIN" PATTERN RUG
Ushak region, western Turkey,
c. 1550–1625
Wool
L. 244 in. (620 cm), w. 106 in. (269 cm)
1985.R.101

TURKEY HAS HAD an important weaving industry for centuries. In the 13th century, Marco Polo traveled through the region and praised its rugs as the most beautiful in the world. By the 15th century, traders were importing Turkish rugs into Europe, where they were extremely expensive and valued as symbols of high rank. For example, Turkish rugs are often depicted in 15th- and 16th-century Italian religious paintings of the enthroned Virgin and Child. In domestic life, these rugs generally were felt to be too precious to serve as floor coverings, and were instead used as exotic tablecloths. This style of rug and those with closely related patterns became so associated with the concept of Middle Eastern rugs in the European consumer's mind that they were copied and adapted in Western weaving centers, especially Spain.

During the 15th and 16th centuries, European artists depicted Turkish rugs with such frequency that collectors have named specific patterns after famous artists, including Hans Memling and Lorenzo Lotto. The Reves rug is of a type known as "Small-Patterned Holbein," named after the German artist Hans Holbein the Younger (1497–1543). This variety is characterized by a central field composed of small octagons. The emblem, or *gul,* is believed to be a tribal symbol and is, as here, frequently decorated with Islamic-style strapwork. In the "Large-Patterned Holbein," the central field contains large octagons aligned vertically. Both "Holbein" types often have Kufesque borders, as in this example, which has patterns along the outer edge resembling the geometric Arabic script called Kufic. Although these patterns are not actually inscriptions, they closely link these rug designs to their Islamic origin.

RUG (DETAIL)
Probably Alcaraz or Cuenca, Spain,
c. 1525–1575
Wool
L. 114 in. (290 cm), w. 63 in. (160 cm)
1985.R.93

SPANISH RUGS REPRESENT one of the oldest extant groups of such textiles. It is believed that Muslim Arabs brought the art of rug weaving to the Iberian Peninsula when they pushed the Visigoths out of Spain in the 8th century. For several centuries thereafter, the finest Spanish rugs were produced by Muslim craftsmen and exported throughout the eastern Mediterranean. The textiles appear to have been especially appreciated in Egypt before Cairo developed a weaving industry of its own.

During the 15th century, Spanish weaving reached its zenith, with several towns in the southwestern region of Murcia producing rugs. Probably made in either Alcaraz or Cuenca, this example reflects the changes that occurred as Muslim craftsmen were supplanted by Christian workers following the defeat of the Moors in 1492. Although the three large octagonal motifs are derived from Turkish rugs imported into Spain, the characteristic octagonal "wheels" of the Islamic prototype have been transformed into "wreaths." By the time this rug was made in the 16th century, Spanish designs had drifted to the point that the original Islamic motifs were highly compromised and mingled with European Gothic and Renaissance patterns. Here, the tracery on the interior of the octagons has little relationship to the highly geometric patterns found on Turkish examples. Also, the non-Islamic border of intertwined griffins was probably inspired by contemporary Spanish or Italian silk designs.

RUG (DETAIL)
Probably Alcaraz, Spain, c. 1525–1575
Silk
L. 197 in. (500 cm), W. 118 in. (300 cm)
1985.R.87

IN THE 16TH CENTURY, as Christian weavers came to dominate the industry, Spanish rug design became increasingly influenced by non-Islamic design sources. The pomegranate and vine motif seen here, for example, was inspired by contemporary Italian and Spanish fabrics. Spanish silks had been well known since the 9th century. As with rugs, early examples were in the Islamic taste and only gradually succumbed to European influences.

At least forty rugs of this pattern are known (Erdmann 1960). This particular example is special because it is one of the few, if not the only one, made of silk. Its survival documents that silk was an option when ordering a Spanish rug, provided the customer was willing to pay for the greater expense of the more precious raw material. The use of silk for this rug also suggests that there may have been closer ties between silk fabric weavers and rug weavers than the simple borrowing of patterns.

RUG (DETAIL)
Murcia region, Spain, c. 1550–1600
Wool
L. 151½ in. (385 cm), w. 88½ in. (225 cm)
1985.R.107

AS IN THE PRECEDING example, the pattern of this rug was derived from contemporary silk fabrics. The pomegranate and vine motif is much more stylized than on the previous rug. Although the design is more crudely rendered, it has a forcefulness that is lacking in the earlier example.

RUG (DETAIL)
Probably Alcaraz, Spain, c. 1550–1600
Wool
L. 146½ in. (372 cm), w. 94½ in. (240 cm)
1985.R.102

THE TOWN OF ALCARAZ, from which this example is believed to have come, rose to prominence as a weaving center in the 15th century. The industry was evidently flourishing by the second half of the century, when the town fathers presented to Queen Isabella of Castile an impressive selection of rugs. By the mid-17th century, however, Alcaraz's industry had all but perished (Kühnel 1953, 3).

Many of the later rugs attributed to Alcaraz are in patterns inspired by contemporary silk fabrics. The lattice with palmette design used here for the center panel is frequently found on Italian voided velvets of the period. Precedents for the border motif of paired beasts confronting one another can be seen in contemporary fabric design.

RUG (DETAIL)
Murcia region, Spain, c. 1600–1650
Wool
L. 126 in. (320 cm), W. 55 in. (140 cm)
1985.R.108

THE SCROLLWORK CONTAINING griffins and urns found in this rug's borders is of Renaissance origin. But the bold baroque design used for the central panel, featuring palmettes contained in oval wreaths of foliage, was popular on 17th-century silk damask fabrics from Italy, Spain, and France. Consequently, this rug cannot date earlier than that period.

Characteristic of later Spanish production is the limited color range found in this rug. While a change in consumer taste could account for this shift, the importation of new dyestuffs, such as cochineal from the New World, as well as the exodus of skilled Jewish dyers, may also have been responsible (Collins 1988, 44).

RUG (DETAIL)
Spain, c. 1600–1650
Wool
L. 146 in. (371 cm), w. 67 in. (170 cm)
1985.R.92

THIS RUG WAS PATTERNED after an imported example from Asia Minor. The central field depicts a garden resplendent with fountains, vases of flowers, and exotic trees, as well as birds, deer, and lions. While "garden" rugs are most often associated with Persia, the borders used here are not. Borders featuring repeating octagons are typically found on rugs from Turkey and the Caucasus. It is possible that the prototype of this rug was made in one of these regions of later production, even though a Persian central motif was utilized.

When Wendy and Emery Reves acquired this rug, it was attributed to the city of Valencia. A Mediterranean port north of Murcia, Valencia is known to have been producing rugs by the 17th century, but as yet none of them can be identified with certainty.

RUG (DETAIL)
Spain or Portugal, 17th century
Wool on linen
L. 136 in. (345 cm), w. 59 in. (150 cm)
1985.R.96

THIS RUG IS part of a large group inspired by Persian medallion rugs. As with many of the imported prototypes, this example contains animal motifs, including birds and leopards. Traditionally attributed to Portugal, this group may contain some rugs of Spanish origin. Regardless of their exact origin, the rugs are embroidered rather than woven.

To create the elaborate pattern, wool yarns were sewn onto a linen ground. This technique was used in various parts of Europe. The Reves Collection contains another example featuring a central medallion that is thought to have been made in southwest France during the 17th century.

RUG (DETAIL)
Possibly Agra, India, c. 1625–1675
Wool
L. 276 in. (701 cm), w. 118 in. (300 cm)
1985.R.110

FOR MANY YEARS, rugs of this type were believed to be of Persian origin. However, scholars now generally agree that this example is part of a group that derived from Persian prototypes but was made in India.

During the 16th and 17th centuries, the Mughal rulers of India prized Persian rugs of similar design and imported them in large numbers for use at their courts. To secure a steady supply, they established weaving centers in the Indian cities of Lahore, Jaipur, and Agra in the 16th century. This example is believed to have come from the famous city of Agra and subsequently to have been exported to Europe. Because of their high-quality design and workmanship, Indian rugs were prized in Europe and were sold there in significant numbers. The fact that countries like Portugal traded extensively with India beginning in the 16th century facilitated this commerce in fine textiles and other Asian luxuries.

RUG
India, 17th century
Wool
L. 114 in. (290 cm), w. 102 in. (259 cm)
1985.R.104

DURING THE LATE 15th and early 16th centuries, the Portuguese acquired trading outposts around the world. In 1482, they built a fort on the Guinea coast of Africa to protect their exportation of slaves, ivory, and gold. Vasco da Gama's renowned expedition around the Cape of Good Hope gave his nation important contacts with the Malindi in East Africa and with the cities of Calicut, Cochin, and Goa in India. This last city became the jewel of the empire.

In 1510, Goa was made the capital of the Portuguese state of India. From this Indian colony, Portugal was able to obtain luxury items unknown to the rest of Europe. It was also able to use the age-old craft traditions of India for the pro-duction of custom products in the Portuguese taste; this rug is such a piece. Made in India in the 17th century, the textile features brightly colored butter-flies, birds, horses, cattle, and flowers in a gardenlike setting. In the center is a double-headed eagle surmounted by a crown. Although the meaning of this particular device is unknown, the double-headed eagle is traditionally associated with the Habsburg family of Austria and Spain. More in keeping with Indian taste is the border motif of carnations and pomegranates. The airy quality of this design and the light-colored ground relate to Indian inlay work in stone and ivory.

"JEPHTHAH'S DAUGHTER" FAN

Possibly England, c. 1740–1750
Skin, gouache, gilding, paint, and ivory
H. 11 in. (27.9 cm), L. 20½ in. (52.1 cm)
1985.R.498

THE FAN FIRST BECAME fashionable in Europe at the court of Henri II of France (r. 1547–1559). While these early fans were useful as cooling devices for the often overdressed and therefore over-heated courtiers, fans had many other functions. As Anna Bennett points out, "They were used, on occasion, as mem-ory aids, for parlor games, or for politi-cal propaganda, as masks, lorgnettes, cryptic communicators, and, of course, accessories in the oldest game, when dalliance was a major preoccupation" (Bennett 1988, 12).

By the 18th century, fans were in use across Europe. Although French artisans and fashion dominated fan design, other countries, including Germany, Italy, and Spain, produced many fine fans. This example is probably English and depicts the Old Testament story of Jephthah's daughter. As is traditional, the biblical figure is shown being greeted by his daughter. He recoils in horror because he has just returned from battle, where he swore to sacrifice the first living thing he sees after a safe return.

The fan's verso depicts a rustic couple with flower baskets. The ivory sticks and guards, which are held in place by a rivet holding a paste jewel, are intricately carved and pierced with Asian-style buildings, temples, and fret-work. Such devices were so fashionable as design elements in the 18th century that the term *chinoiserie* was coined to describe the vogue.

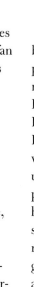

"THE CARD GAME" FAN
France, c. 1740–1750
Skin, gouache, paint, and ivory
H. 11 in. (27.9 cm), W. 20¼ in. (51.4 cm)
1985.R.494

THROUGHOUT THE 18th century, scenes of daily life were extremely popular as fan motifs. The Reves Collection contains several fine examples of this genre, including this fan. Here, the painter has depicted well-dressed members of the upper class in various leisure pursuits inside a grand rococo-style interior. In the center, three play at cards; others read or frolic with pets. To the left is a stool supporting sheet music and a lute, representing the enjoyment of music. Flanking this central scene are two vignettes of children exploring the outdoors. The division of the fan leaf's surface into multiple areas is typical of many examples made at mid-century or later. This practice allowed the painter to depict various aspects of daily life simultaneously. On this fan, the theme of play is carried out by both children and adults side by side.

The fan's verso is painted with floral borders, while its sticks and guards are pierced and painted with symbols of romantic love. The central figures are Hercules and Omphale, queen of Lydia. Having completed his twelve labors, Hercules agrees to sell himself into slavery for one year in order to find peace upon his return to Thebes. Omphale purchases Hercules and has him serve her as a lover. Supposedly, Omphale so dominated the manly Hercules that rumors reached Greece that he had begun to dress as a woman and to weave and spin with the queen's attendants. Consequently, Hercules is traditionally depicted with a spindle when in the presence of Omphale, as here. To emphasize the romantic nature of Hercules and the queen's relationship, the scene on these sticks is filled with cherubs, butterflies, and flowers.

"THE BUSTLING BRIDGE" FAN

France, c. 1750–1760
Paper, gouache, and ivory
H. 10½ in. (26.7 cm), w. 19 in. (48.3 cm)
1985.R.508

THIS FAN IS ESPECIALLY interesting for its elaborate depiction of city life. The background is a view of a great European capital. Cleverly fitted to the curved format, a bridge bustling with activity arches across the foreground. On the left is an apple seller. Next to her is a figure who points to a banner while addressing the public. This scene, together with the uniformed officer on horseback at the far right, may depict military recruitment or opposing political factions. The set-ting is further enlivened with coaches and cabriolets, along with various vendors, pedestrians, and soldiers.

The sticks feature painted vases of flowers and a courting couple in low relief. The rivet holding the sticks together is set with a paste jewel. The ivory guards are carved with flowers, birds, a girl, and a boy. On the leaf's verso is a view of a funerary monument with three figures strolling nearby.

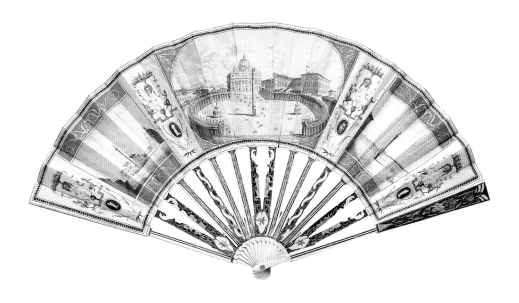

"ST. PETER'S BASILICA" FAN

Italy, c. 1785–1790
Skin, gouache, bone, and silver and gold gilt
H. 11 in. (27.9 cm), w. 20¼ in. (51.4 cm)
1985.R.519

ROME, FAMOUS FOR its architecture, was a requisite stop on the Grand Tour during the 18th century. To commemorate their arrival in the Eternal City, many travelers purchased fans that depicted famous Roman attractions. The central reserve on this fan features St. Peter's Basilica with its forecourt and Bernini colonnades. The monuments depicted to either side are likely the columns of Trajan and Marcus Aurelius. The views were probably adapted from one of the many engravings of the monuments of Rome done by artists like Giovanni Battista Piranesi. Separating the scenes are Pompeiian-style panels with cameos. The verso is simply decorated with sprigs of flowers. The rivet joining the sticks holds a paste jewel.

Furniture

Wendy and Emery Reves acquired several exceptional examples of European furniture, although they did not focus their collecting in this area. Much of the furniture used by the couple was already in situ at Villa La Pausa when they purchased the estate in 1953. During the period when Coco Chanel and the Duke of Westminster occupied the villa, a significant amount of 16th- and 17th-century-style furniture was shipped to the house from one of the duke's numerous English homes. Many of these furnishings, however, were in a poor state of preservation when the Reveses came to La Pausa. Nevertheless, Wendy Reves decided to restore the pieces rather than replace them, and to that end she converted a garage on the property into a workshop so that she could oversee the conservation.

During the ensuing decades, the Reveses purchased relatively little furniture in comparison to porcelain, glass, and ironwork. Those pieces they did acquire were obtained in various locales. Of the examples illustrated here, for example, the Italian stand came from Luigi Orselli in Florence, and the pair of torchères was acquired in 1963 from Arturo Linares in Madrid. Emery Reves purchased both cabinets-on-stands in 1967 as birthday gifts for his wife. Although Antoine Perpitch in Paris sold them to Reves, there were evidently two other investors in the ivory cabinet; their names were Litybur and Lagrand.

Perhaps the most interesting aspect of the Reves furniture acquisitions is the sizable group of mid-19th-century English papier-mâché pieces. The collecting of such objects was extremely avant-garde on the part of Wendy Reves. During the 1960s, when she was building the collection, the ornate rococo revival style was in great disrepute. Nevertheless, Reves, working through galleries like La Boutique du Village in Paris and Stair & Co. in London, gathered together more than twenty examples, most of which are now at the Dallas Museum of Art. The collection is especially noteworthy because of its wide variety of forms.

STAND

Central Italy, probably Florence,
c. 1650–1700
Pine, paint, and gilding
H. 48 in. (121.9 cm), W. 20½ in. (52.1 cm),
D. 21 in. (53.3 cm)
1985.R.618

STANDS SUCH AS THIS example were
popular furniture forms among the
wealthy in 17th-century Italy. Because
they were lightweight, stands could be
moved about as required to support
candelabra, sculpture, and other decorative objects in the huge rooms and hall-
ways that were typical of much domestic
and public architecture of the period.
Like many surviving examples believed
to have been made in central Italy, this
one features grotesque winged masks at
top and bottom and stands on paw feet.
The Reveses purchased this stand in
Florence from Luigi Orselli, who believed it had been made in that city.

TORCHERE (ONE OF A PAIR)

Probably Spain, c. 1725–1775
Gilt wood
H. 64½ in. (163.8 cm), W. 27 in. (68.6 cm),
D. 27 in. (68.6 cm)
1985.R.619

LIKE THE PRECEDING STAND, torchères were popular because they could easily be moved to wherever light was needed. They typically either had flat tops to support candelabra or sockets into which candles were placed. Originally, the Reves examples terminated in a single large socket.

The combination of a triangular base, turned central shaft, and circular top developed in Italy during the 16th and 17th centuries. This Iberian example is heavily influenced by Italian prototypes. However, the exuberant scrollwork and the garlands of flowers point to a mid-18th-century date, when the rococo style dominated European design. Furthermore, the radiant heart on the base indicates that this example and its mate were made for an ecclesiastical setting. Torchères were often used to flank altars in churches and private chapels.

CABINET-ON-STAND

Probably Paris, France; possibly Antwerp,
Belgium, c. 1650–1675
Wood, tortoiseshell, ivory, and gilt bronze
H. 67⅝ in. (171.8 cm), W. 56¾ in. (144.1 cm),
D. 20½ in. (52.1 cm)
1985.R.574.a–c

DURING THE FIRST HALF of the 17th century, the cabinet-on-stand became an important furniture form in Italy. Not only were such cabinets useful for the storage of small personal articles and collectibles but they could be highly decorative. Italian examples were especially noteworthy because they were often covered with *pietre dure* marquetry. In this technique, hard stones selected for their color were shaped so that they could be assembled like a puzzle into decorative motifs and glued onto the surface of a piece of furniture. By the mid-17th century, clients in northern Europe were demanding furniture decorated in this fashion. While some Italian furniture with *pietre dure,* as well as ready-made stone slabs, were imported, cabinetmakers in various parts of Europe created acceptable alternatives to the Italian prototypes.

This cabinet is a fine example of such work. It is close to Italian examples in its overall form, a case containing banks of drawers supported on an open frame. However, instead of using stone veneer to achieve colorful effects, the surface is faced with marquetry composed of tortoiseshell, ivory, and various natural and dyed woods. Nevertheless, the nature of the wooden marquetry is quite close to *pietre dure* examples, as it is composed of relatively large elements arranged in stiff patterns. Also linking this example closely to Italian prototypes are the motifs of flowers and birds arranged on alternating drawers, a formula that frequently appears on Italian work. This affinity to Italian prototypes suggests that the cabinet may have been made in the 1650s or 1660s, soon after the vogue for polychrome floral marquetry reached northern Europe.

At present, the exact origin of this cabinet is unknown. Th. H. Scheurleer has argued convincingly that the cabinet-on-stand form was being made in Paris by the early 1650s (Scheurleer 1984, 333). As Scheurleer points out, however, cabinetmakers in Antwerp were making and exporting the form by the mid-1650s. Consequently, it is difficult to prove conclusively that this example is Parisian. Only a systematic analysis of the construction features of a large group of related cabinets is likely to answer such questions.

The intercolumnar elements beneath the drawer section of the frame are either replacements or relatively recent additions.

CABINET-ON-STAND

Probably Pierre Gole (c. 1620–1684), Paris,
France, c. 1660–1680
Wood, tortoiseshell, ivory, shell, and gilt bronze
H. 68¼ in. (173.4 cm), W. 49½ in. (125.7 cm),
D. 17 in. (43.2 cm)
1985.R.573.a–c

THIS CABINET IS CLOSELY related in form to the preceding example, but its decoration is much more sophisticated. Whereas the marquetry on the other cabinet is stiffly arranged and composed of largish elements, these patterns are complicated, naturalistic, and technically superior. Here, the woodworker used a veneer saw guided by a template to produce hundreds of intricate elements. To achieve a sense of realism, these pieces were shaded in hot sand and dyed various colors before being assembled into bouquets and garlands of flowers. The wooden elements were then set into a background veneer of ivory surrounded by bands created from crushed mother-of-pearl set in mastic. The combination of colored woods, white ivory, and reflective shell ensured that this cabinet glistened like a jewel in the dim candlelight of the 17th century.

Because the underside of each drawer in this cabinet carries a French inscription denoting its proper location in the case, and because it is known that ivory-veneered furniture was made in Paris, this example can be assigned to

Paris with relative certainty. In fact, since Pierre Gole was the only cabinetmaker recorded in the royal building records as producing marquetry on an ivory ground, the Reves cabinet has been attributed to Gole by Th. H. Scheurleer (Scheurleer 1985). If this example is the work of Louis XIV's master cabinet-maker, then a comparison with another ivory cabinet attributed to Gole and believed to have been made for the king's brother, Philippe d'Orléans, indicates that there was a wide range in the quality of marquetry produced in Gole's shop. Compared to the Reves cabinet, the marquetry on the Orléans cabinet, now in the Victoria and Albert Museum, London, is crudely cut and closer to *pietre dure* work in its stiffness. Perhaps the Reves example was created long enough after the Orléans one (c. 1662) for Gole and his workmen to perfect their marquetry techniques and move beyond the static *pietre dure* style. Or perhaps the cabinets are contemporary, with the Reves marquetry having been made by a more skilled craftsman.

The gilt feet are replacements.

TWO BOXES

Spa, Belgium, c. 1675–1725
Wood, lacquer, mother-of-pearl, and brass
H. (top) 5 in. (12.7 cm), W. 14 in. (35.6 cm),
D. 9¾ in. (24.8 cm); H. (bottom) 5 in. (12.7 cm),
W. 12½ in. (31.8 cm), D. 9 in. (22.9 cm)
1985.R.465, 446

THESE BOXES ARE EXAMPLES of inlay and lacquer work done in the French-speaking town of Spa, near Liège. As early as the 14th century, Spa was known for the curative powers of its waters and hence developed into a gathering place for Europe's elite. Simultaneously, a trade in souvenirs sprang up. Local craftspersons produced a wide range of goods, including walking sticks, bowls, brushes, watch cases, trays, and tobacco boxes, which were purchased by tourists and thereby distributed throughout the continent. By the late 17th century, Spa was known for objects, like these boxes, that featured decorations in mother-of-pearl, ivory, pewter, copper, brass, and silver set on lacquered wood grounds (Huth 1971, 107–8).

These boxes belong to a sizable group, many of which appear to have been purchased by English tourists. With their flowers, birds, and scrolls, the boxes are characteristic of late 17th-century baroque decoration. However, the stiffness and stylization of the mother-of-pearl work and the inclusion of exotic birds like parrots suggest Indian influence. The trading center of Goa on the west coast of India was famous for the shell and ivory inlay work it exported to Europe from the 15th century on. Furthermore, Indian inlay was highly influential throughout the Philippines and Indonesia. Since the Dutch East India Company maintained a base in Jakarta beginning in the early 17th century, it is not unreasonable to believe that the inlay workers of Spa had access to imported products from India and the Pacific Rim and were influenced by them.

The central boss on one box (facing page, bottom) depicts a dog chasing a rabbit. The other bears the English coat of arms of Baron Willoughby of Parham (see detail). The motto reads *Virtue sans Peur* (Virtue without Fear).

The four corner ovals engraved with the initials *BEW* are probably replacements dating to the late 18th century. The feet on both boxes are additions.

CHEST
Probably Spain, c. 1625–1725
Rosewood, ebony, ivory, and gilt metal
H. 13⅝ in. (34.6 cm), W. 18¾ in. (47.6 cm),
D. 11¾ in. (29.8 cm)
1985.R.605

THIS CHEST WAS PURCHASED by the Reveses in Madrid and is likely to have been made there. Although its origin is uncertain, the sophisticated use of exotic imported woods suggests an Iberian provenance. Following the exploration of Central America by the Spanish in the 1490s and of the east coast of Africa and Brazil by the Portuguese in the first decade of the 16th century, exotic materials like ebony, rosewood, and ivory became increasingly available to Iberian woodworkers. Because of restrictive trading laws, Spanish and Portuguese craftsmen were able to make objects from such luxurious materials before the rest of their continental counterparts. However, because the Habsburg Empire controlled much of the Low Countries as well as Spain and Portugal between the 1580s and 1713, cabinetmakers in centers like Antwerp were soon able to work in these materials. And as trade in colonial raw materials widened, workers throughout Europe eventually had access to exotic woods and animal products.

BOX
Jennens & Bettridge, Birmingham, England,
c. 1830–1860
Papier-mâché, lacquer, paint, and mother-of-pearl
H. 2⅛ in. (5.4 cm), W. 11⅞ in. (30.2 cm),
D. 10¼ in. (26 cm)
1985.R.469.a–l

THE FRENCH TERM *papier-mâché* refers to pulped paper mixed with an adhesive and shaped in molds, but the 19th-century English material was made differently. It was created by gluing together sheets of paper over a form that could be further shaped with a lathe, rasp, or plane. In 1772, Henry Clay of Birmingham evidently invented this technique and patented it in that year. However, it was Jennens & Bettridge, the successor firm to Clay's, that greatly extended the range and quality of this type of work. By the 1850s, the firm was producing numerous forms, including chairs, tables, cabinets, bookcases, bedsteads, pianoforte cases, and boxes. Besides the wide spectrum of its wares, Jennens & Bettridge was also known for its mother-of-pearl decoration. In 1825, George Souter, one of the firm's employees, introduced pearl-shell inlaying (Symonds 1962, 195–99). Although the technique was used by others, Jennens & Bettridge appears to have made many of the finest articles of this type and is probably responsible for several of the other pieces illustrated here. Nevertheless, this box featuring a fanciful chinoiserie scene and five lidded interior compartments is the only documented example. The verso is stamped *JENNENS & BETTRIDGE*.

SIDE CHAIR
Probably Birmingham or Wolverhampton,
England, c. 1830–1860
Papier-mâché, wood, cane, lacquer, paint,
mother-of-pearl, and gilding
H. 34½ in. (87.6 cm), W. 24½ in. (62.2 cm),
D. 28 in. (71.1 cm)
1985.R.633

DURING THE SECOND quarter of the 19th century, English craftspersons made a wide range of objects that were decorated with paint and mother-of-pearl. Some of the furniture, especially that constructed of papier-mâché, was innovative in terms of its material and shape. The flared back of this chair, for example, would be difficult to create in wood but could easily be shaped using pliable sheets of paper. Because papier-mâché damages easily when under stress, most of this furniture has wooden or metal supporting elements. Some is even entirely constructed from wood but decorated in papier-mâché. This chair has a wooden seat frame to which the wooden legs and caning are attached.

The vogue for furniture decorated with dark lacquer, shell, and paint lasted into the mid-19th century. In 1860, for example, the two main centers of production, Birmingham and Wolverhampton, employed between 1,000 and 2,000 craftspersons making this line of furniture and related articles (Joy 1977, 272).

TILT-TOP TABLE
Probably Birmingham or Wolverhampton, England,
c. 1830–1860
Wood, lacquer, paint, mother-of-pearl, gilding, and
possibly papier-mâché
H. (top down) 38½ in. (97.8 cm), DIAM. 33 in. (83.8 cm)
1985.R.627

THE FACT THAT THE TOP of this table tilts up suggests that as late as the mid-19th century furniture was still regularly removed from the center of a room when not in use and placed against the wall. Furthermore, the practice of tilting up the top allowed elaborately painted tables to function like a painting on an easel. This particular example is especially elaborate. Its central motif was achieved by inlaying pieces of mother-of-pearl into what might be a thin layer of papier-mâché over a wood substrate. Layers of paint and varnish were then applied atop the shell, producing lustrous flowers and birds, which were popular decorative motifs in 19th-century design. The table was further animated with finely painted gilt bands and scrollwork.

BED HEADBOARD
Probably Birmingham or Wolverhampton,
England, c. 1830–1860
Papier-mâché, lacquer, paint, mother-of-pearl,
gilding, and metal
H. 57¾ in. (146.7 cm), W. 55⅝ in. (141.3 cm),
D. 2¾ in. (7 cm)
1985.R.649

THIS HEADBOARD IS PART of an exceptionally fine bed. Bedsteads decorated in this fashion are rare because of their fragility. The posts are painted metal with brass finials and mounts. The headboard is papier-mâché covered with lacquer, paint, and gilding. Horizontal iron strips on its back prevent warping and add strength. The wisteria blossoms that hang down from the crest were created by gluing on hundreds of small pieces of mother-of-pearl.

Because such ornament required much handwork, its production was championed by those interested in promoting handicrafts. By 1852, for example, England's Department of Practical Art, which later became the Victoria and Albert Museum, London, owned twenty-two examples of papier-mâché and lacquered furniture (Aslin 1962, 46). One of the few other beds of the quality seen here is in the Victoria and Albert Museum.

CANTERBURY

Probably Birmingham or Wolverhampton, England,
c. 1830–1860
Papier-mâché, wood, lacquer, paint, mother-of-
pearl, and gilding
H. 26 in. (66 cm), W. 27¾ in. (70.5 cm), D. 16 in.
(40.6 cm)
1985.R.642

CANTERBURIES WERE DEVELOPED in the late 18th and early 19th centuries to hold printed matter like sheet music and magazines. While numerous examples survive in a variety of materials, including cast iron, canterburies incorporating papier-mâché are rare because the weight of bound sheet music and periodicals weakened the paper elements over time and eventually destroyed them.

Besides being rare, the Reves example is noteworthy for its strongly scrolled form. Beginning in the 1820s and 1830s, European and American designers returned to the rococo ornament of the second quarter of the 18th century for inspiration. Rather than copy these airy curvilinear forms and patterns, 19th-century craftspersons gave their objects heavier proportions with bolder curves, as in this example. This style of ornament is known today as rococo revival.

DRESSING MIRROR

Probably Birmingham or Wolverhampton,
England, c. 1830–1860
Wood, papier-mâché, lacquer, paint,
mother-of-pearl, gilding, and brass
H. 35⅛ in. (89.2 cm), w. 30½ in.
(77.5 cm), D. 14½ in. (36.8 cm)
1985.R.636

THIS DRESSING MIRROR is exceedingly well decorated. The base and the mirror's crest are ornamented with westernized views of Asia. Since the initiation of regular trade with China in the 16th and 17th centuries, Europeans had been fascinated with imported luxury goods like tea, porcelain, and silk. Simultaneously, Westerners also fantasized about what Asian cultures were like and developed an entire decorative style known today as chinoiserie. The pagodalike structures seen here had been used on European furniture for 200 years before they were applied to this piece.

The construction of this dressing mirror is complicated. The base is made of papier-mâché from sheets of paper. By allowing the paper to dry over a mold, the maker achieved the curve of the base's skirt. Since greater strength was needed to support the heavy mirror glass, wooden uprights were used. Because all these materials expand and contract at different rates, thereby causing damage, few complex pieces such as this survive.

Frames

While his wife appreciated them, frames were the passion of Emery Reves. He seems to have become interested in the subject as part of collecting paintings. Since he purchased many of the pictures in London, it was only natural for him to acquire frames in that city as well. To that end, the renowned firm of Arnold Wiggins and Sons, Ltd., was pivotal. Ever inquisitive, Emery Reves occasionally examined frames offered by other dealers, but it was through Wiggins that he acquired the vast majority of his collection.

Long before frame connoisseurship was of interest to collectors or art historians, Emery Reves had gained great knowledge in this specialty. Wiggins employees who knew Reves note that when in London he typically spent entire days examining frames and speaking with craftsmen. This rapport resulted in especially fine frames being put aside for Reves's inspection before they were offered to others. For many years, Reves kept all his frame purchases in storage at Wiggins's warehouse. Only as paintings were acquired and subsequently reframed did the collection begin to find its way to Villa La Pausa. In 1971, the Wiggins firm was forced to move its warehouse, and Reves took this opportunity to remove the thirty frames stored in London to the south of France. Once at the villa, many of the frames were never used to surround paintings but were simply admired as great examples of the carver's art.

The Reves frame collection is extremely fine and diverse. It contains examples from England, Italy, Austria, Germany, Spain, and the Netherlands. However, its great strength is in French frames, as illustrated by several of the following entries.

PICTURE FRAME

Probably Venice, Italy, c. 1550
Gilt pine
H. 34⅞ in. (88.6 cm), w. 29½ in. (74.9 cm),
D. 3½ in. (8.9 cm)
1985.R.79.b

THE INDEPENDENT EASEL picture was an Italian invention of the 15th century and quickly came to dominate the idea of "art" propagated in the Renaissance. In order to house these new portable "illusions," an equally new kind of furniture was developed. The picture frame is now so ubiquitous that one forgets that, like all familiar forms, it was an invention. Although frames were originally conceived to protect the picture physically and enhance it aesthetically, their invention led gradually to the creation of a separate type of craft associated more often with furniture making than with the creation of pictures themselves.

This particular frame is in exceptionally good condition. Its fine state was undoubtedly one of the reasons why it was included in the most important frame exhibition of the 20th century, held in Paris at the Galerie Georges Petit in 1931 (Petit 1931, no. 524). The frame preserves its original format, having never been cut down or enlarged for another painting. The simple delicacy of its proportions and its fine carving suggest that it housed an important work of art, which most probably had complex forms and colors that needed to be offset by a simple surround. Frames like this one are often called "Giorgione frames" because they relate to the simple surrounds created for the precious religious and allegorical paintings of the most important Venetian painter of the Renaissance, Giorgio del Castelfranco.

CRESTED MIRROR FRAME

France, Flanders, or Holland, c. 1660
Gilt oak
H. 57 in. (144.8 cm), W. 37 in. (94 cm),
D. 7 in. (17.8 cm)
1985.R.407

MIRRORS WERE OFTEN as valuable and important as paintings in 16th- and early 17th-century interiors and were frequently framed even more elaborately than pictures. This superb mirror frame is of a type produced in Italy, France, Flanders, and England in the mid-17th century for aristocratic or upper-middle-class interiors. The design called for two separately carved and gilded components, a rectangular frame for the mirror itself and an elaborate crest. In certain cases, the crests enable us to identify the owner of the frame, either by a coat of arms or by a combination of heraldic symbols commonly associated with a particular family. In this case, the cherubs that dominate the center of the floral crest flank a shield that has no coat of arms, suggesting that the frame was either made for stock or once had a painted coat of arms that is now lost. Its technique and style relate it most clearly to mirror frames produced in France.

MIRROR OR PORTRAIT FRAME

Probably Lyons, France, c. 1630
Gilt oak
H. 47 in. (119.4 cm), W. 39 in. (99 cm),
D. 2 in. (5 cm)
1985.R.405

THIS FRAME WAS CARVED for a sumptuous interior in the Italianate French city of Lyons sometime in the first half of the 17th century. Its classicized forms include many from the standard repertoire of Roman decorative designs—acanthus and grape leaves, nude children, bunches of grapes, and dolphins. Although dolphins appear in Italian frames of the same period, they are much more common in France, where they are associated with the crown prince, or "dauphin," a symbol of the endurance of the French monarchy. Here, the dolphins not only cavort with the children on the sides of the frame but curl lovingly into the contours of a wicker basket that once may have held carved or gilt plaster flowers on wire stems. All of the forms in the frame suggest abundance, power, and pleasure.

This frame has long been associated with Lyons, the seat of the immense French textile industry and the city whose position on the Rhone linked it directly to both the Mediterranean and Paris, the administrative center of France. The frame itself is of a type called *cassetta,* which originated in Italy, but its persistent use of the dolphin, the particular mode of carving, and the fact that it is made of oak suggest northern origins.

PICTURE FRAME

France, c. 1650
Gilt oak
H. 14⅝ in. (37.1 cm), W. 17⅝ in. (44.8 cm),
D. 1½ in. (3.8 cm)
1985.R.35.b

ELABORATE FRAMES CARVED for portraits or mirrors exist in greater quantity than do the physically fragile and adaptable frames made for small paintings or drawings. Thus, it is remarkable that this elegant frame survives almost unscathed, with its original dimensions, if not its subtle gilded surface, preserved. Like many frames of the late 16th and early 17th centuries, it adapts its shape to both the wall on which it rested and the picture it protected, as it rises in profile from the picture to its greatest height

and then gradually recedes through smaller carved crests and gilded valleys until it meets the plane of the wall. Each of the four ornamental bands is placed on a different plane, and each contrasts in motif and rhythm so as to pick up and distribute light, creating a gentle penumbra around the missing image.

Nearest the work of art is a spiral of gilded ribbon that must have challenged the frame's carver as he created a continuous curve in the grainy oak. Next are two bands of repetitive decorations. The most elaborate of the bands has frilly acanthus leaves that seem to sprout from the frame and grow in the direction of the wall, curling back at the very end to return our attention to the picture.

PICTURE FRAME
France, c. 1660–1710
Gilt limewood
H. 17 in. (43.2 cm), W. 22 in. (55.9 cm),
D. 1⅞ in. (4.8 cm)
1985.R.360

THIS SMALL FRAME was probably carved in Paris sometime during the last years of the 17th century or the early 18th century. The proportions of the opening and the fact that the frame has no cartouches on the smaller sides suggest that it was made for a horizontal painting, perhaps a landscape. The quality of the carving is very high, especially in the separately conceived overlapping acanthus leaves that seem to grow over the edge of the frame toward the central opening. Like many frames produced in France during this period, this one is thickest and most substantial at the outside, creating a certain bulk for the framed object and thereby giving it the status of furniture or architecture when hung. It could certainly have been carved to be placed in the private chamber of a wealthy collector whose taste ran to small-scale works.

PICTURE FRAME
France, c. 1700
Gilt oak
H. 73¼ in. (186 cm), W. 63½ in. (161.3 cm),
D. 7 in. (17.8 cm)
1985.R.374

THIS FRAME IS AMONG the finest early
18th-century frames in the collection.
Although it has lost a small portion of
the cartouche at the bottom center
(which would have looked like those on
the left and right sides), it is otherwise
in a fine state, having never been adapted
to fit another work of art and having
never been regilded or resurfaced to play
a role in an updated interior. The intertwined *L* motif in the top center cartouche suggests that the frame originally
held a royal portrait or, less likely, that
it was carved for an important vertical
painting in the French royal collection.

If the latter is true, the frame was probably originally hung in one of the palaces
in or near Paris—the Louvre, the Tuile-
ries, Versailles, Marly-le-Roi, or Saint-
Germain-des-Pres.

Like all French frames made during
the second half of the 17th and the early
18th centuries, this one has its greatest
thickness along the outside and makes
its most exuberant decorative gestures
at the corners and midpoints of each
side. An "inner frame" covers the edges
of the stretcher and appears to be held in
place by a variety of tendrils, carved in
high relief and occasionally in full relief,
that grow in great rhythmic curves from
the corner cartouches. These powerful
vines have a counterpoint in the low-
relief floral vegetation that runs behind
them, which has its most splendid elabo-
ration on the four corners. The central
cartouches each approximate architecture, with their carved grids and brackets
suggesting furniture and moldings.

What is particularly splendid about
this frame is its surface, which combines
oil and water gilding for greater variety
and sparkle. The undersides and the
smooth concave surface between the
inner and outer frames are oil gilded and
highly burnished so that they shine almost like a golden mirror. The complex
areas of relief are water gilded, probably
on white or yellow gesso, producing a
lighter surface of more matte quality that
permits easy visual comprehension of
the complex carving. To give extra visual
drama to the whole, the gilder picked
out certain details to oil gild—repeated
carved balls and other ovoid or spherical
shapes—and then burnished these so
that they glow like pearls amid the tex-
tured wealth of water-gilded vegetation.
Any royal sitter would have had added
luster when he or she commanded from
within this masterpiece of carving and
gilding.

THREE FRAGMENTS OF A PICTURE FRAME

France, c. 1700
Gilt oak
H. (top) 12¼ in. (31.1 cm), L. 73½ in. (186.7 cm),
D. 7 in. (17.8 cm); H. (middle) 11 in. (27.9 cm),
L. 73¾ in. (187.3 cm), D. 7 in. (17.8 cm);
H. (bottom) 11½ in. (29.2 cm), L. 40⅜ in. (102.5 cm),
D. 7 in. (17.8 cm)
1985.R.404.a–c

THESE THREE FRAGMENTS are all that remains of one of the great French frames made at the very end of the reign of Louis XIV or early in the reign of his grandson, Louis XV. In their present state, they falsely suggest that frames were made in large sections for stock and then assembled afterward to fit particular pictures. In fact, exactly the opposite was the case. When a frame was needed for a work in the royal collection, a design was created that took into account the particular picture and the decoration of the room in which it would hang. A great cabinetmaker or specialized frame maker would then commence work. A joiner would assemble large pieces of cured wood to fit the specific dimensions and would ready the piece for the carver, who would work directly in the wood from designs prepared either by a cabinet-maker, an artist, or an architect. These designs would be calibrated not only to harmonize with the picture itself, but, more important, to take their part in a richly carved and furnished room. The carved frame would be covered with a coat of gesso or fine plaster and recarved. A master gilder would then analyze the form and surface textures of the frame and design a pattern of water and oil gild-ing that best suited it. In certain cases, the frame was gilded simultaneously with the major pieces of furniture and the pan-eling for a room.

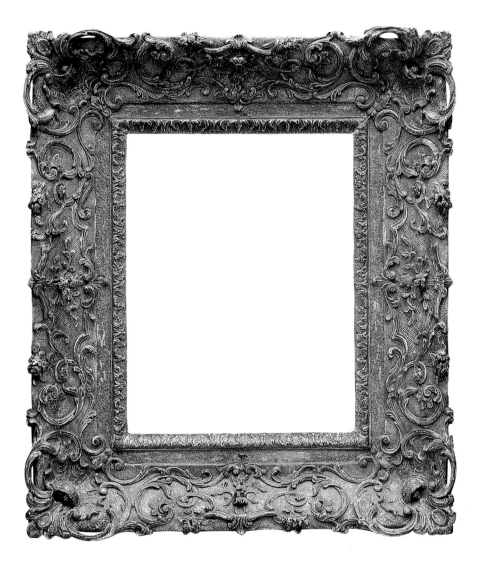

PICTURE FRAME

France, c. 1720
Gilt oak
H. 15½ in. (39.4 cm), w. 13⅜ in. (34 cm),
D. 2¼ in. (5.7 cm)
1985.R.37.b

THIS SMALL OAK FRAME is in a fine state of preservation. Although it maintains the center and corner cartouche common in French frames of the second half of the 17th and the early 18th centuries, the carving of tendrils and scrolls pulls all elements of the frame together so that it would form a continuous decorated surface around the work of art it contained. Interestingly, this carved oak frame also preserves its original gilded surface as well as a good deal of the subtle ornament recarved by the master carver in the coat of gesso applied over the carved wooden form.

The size of this frame indicates that it may have been commissioned by one of the great 18th-century Parisian connoisseurs of drawings, many of whom were vying with each other to acquire major works in ink, pencil, chalk, and charcoal by the greatest French and Italian masters of the Renaissance and baroque periods. The subtle delicacy of this frame and the generalized rhythms of its carving would no doubt have been appropriate to a great drawing by Raphael, Perugino, or Claude Lorrain.

PICTURE FRAME

France, c. 1740
Gilt oak
H. 18¾ in. (47.6 cm), W. 17¾ in. (45 cm),
D. 4 in. (10.2 cm)
1985.R.378

THE QUALITY OF THE CARVING on this small frame makes it one of the masterpieces in the collection. Yet its unusually squat proportions indicate that it might have been cut down from a larger frame. The sheer concentration of ornamental motifs and the heaviness of the frame suggest either that it was made to house a small painting of unusual importance or that it was subtly re-created from the corners and the top and bottom centers of a larger frame. Whatever its origin, the frame is of great richness and must have enshrined a small work of art of real significance to its 18th-century owner. The scale of the ornamental carving is such that it would have overpowered even the greatest of drawings, and given the prominence of the top central cartouche, it is more likely that the frame was conceived—or reconfigured—to contain a portrait.

PICTURE FRAME

France, c. 1750
Gilt oak
H. 26¼ in. (66.7 cm), w. 23 in. (58.4 cm),
D. 2⅞ in. (7.3 cm)
64.1985.b

THIS ROCOCO FRAME is among the finest in the United States. Although it employs the standard corner and center format, the quality of its carving is so high that it must have been commissioned by a major patron for a great work of art to be housed in an important room. The combination of shells, scrolls, flowers, leaves, and branches that swirl rhythmically around the center is intoxicating, and there are so few repetitions of form

that one is never bored looking at this frame. Since most French furniture of this period was based on curvilinear principles of design, the challenge for a frame maker was to transform a simple rectangular opening into a symphony of curves that undulate in space so as to engage in a subtle conversation with the arms of chairs, the ormolu mounts on commodes, or the legs of tables. The maker's success in the conception and execution of this frame is total; one can easily imagine it surrounding a portrait by Jean-Marc Nattier or Jean-Honoré Fragonard.

Glass

In total, the Reves holdings in glass number over 200. The majority of these pieces are Spanish and likely come from the La Granja factory. Wendy Reves was especially interested in the medium and acquired much glass while traveling in Spain during the 1960s and early 1970s. Examples of central European and French glass, including the cruet set illustrated here, were purchased from Philippe Leroux in Paris in the 1960s. In 1971, the large French candlestick was acquired from Joseph & Earle D. Vandekar in London. Some of the rarest English glass, such as the sweetmeat dish with looped rim and the engraved covered goblet, came from Cecil Davis, Ltd., in 1969.

BOTTLE

Venice, Italy, c. 1650–1700
Nonlead glass and pewter
H. 8½ in. (21.6 cm), DIAM. 4⁵⁄₁₆ in. (11 cm)
1985.R.169.a–b

VENICE SUPPORTED GLASS furnaces as early as the 11th century. By the 13th century, they had grown so numerous that city officials became concerned about possible fires and restricted glass-making to the island of Murano, where it still resides. During the ensuing centuries, Venice's artisans excelled so in both design and technique that their wares were exported throughout Europe. Until at least the 17th century, Venice was unrivaled as Europe's foremost producer of fine tablewares.

Venetian glass is exceptionally diverse. From an early date, workers there produced both clear and colored glass. This bottle is a fine example of chalcedony, or *calcedonio,* glass. Like much of Venice's colored glass, this type imitated a semiprecious stone. Gemstones and rock crystal were highly prized materials, and therefore glass that imitated them was also coveted. Chalcedony glass was first made in Venice in the late 15th century. However, its popularity continued during the next 200 years. In fact, it was exported to such an extent throughout Europe that flasks of this type were thought to have been made in France and Germany when they were actually Venetian imports.

FOOTED SALVER
Venice, Italy, 17th century
Nonlead glass
H. 3¾ in. (9.5 cm), w. 8½ in. (21.6 cm)
1985.R.194

THE STRIPED DECORATION on the top surface of this salver is characteristic of Venetian work. This type of ornament is known as *vetro a retorti,* or "glass with twists." Developed during the Renaissance, the style remained popular through the 18th century. It is made by applying glass canes with opaque glass twists to the clear glass. As the hot glass is worked, the round canes are flattened into the surface to form the pattern. In this example, canes of solid color were also used to achieve a pattern of alternating stripes.

This form and the related cup-shaped tazza were produced in large numbers by Venetian glasshouses. While both forms held food of various kinds, footed salvers could also be used to elevate other vessels. For example, they are known to have held sets of glasses.

BOTTLE

France, c. 1700–1750
Nonlead glass
H. 13⅝ in. (34.6 cm), w. 8 1/16 in. (20.5 cm),
D. 5⅛ in. (13 cm)
1985.R.177

AS IN MANY EUROPEAN countries, glass-making began in France under Roman occupation. During the Middle Ages, France became known for its production of stained glass for ecclesiastical architecture. As late as the 18th century, it was most famous for its fine plate and window glass, a factory for which had been established in 1693 at Saint-Gobain. French table- and decorative ware is less well known. Nevertheless, French artisans did produce some notable domestic glass at centers like Orléans, Rouen, and Nantes.

The primary product of France's glass industry was bottles, the vast major-ity of which were purely functional, having no decoration. A few, however, were ornamented in some way. Here, for example, a glob affixed to the bottle's side was impressed with a fleur-de-lys. Furthermore, to create fluted sides, the molten glass was blown into a ribbed mold. Once removed, the glass bubble was expanded, spreading out the ribs. Finally, to make the bottle stable when sitting, a foot rim was added around the base. The marks of the glassworker's tools were imprinted around this rim. The glass ring around the top of the neck was used as an anchor around which string was tied to secure a stopper.

Because of their heavy use, bottles of this age are rare. At present, only a handful of examples like this one are known.

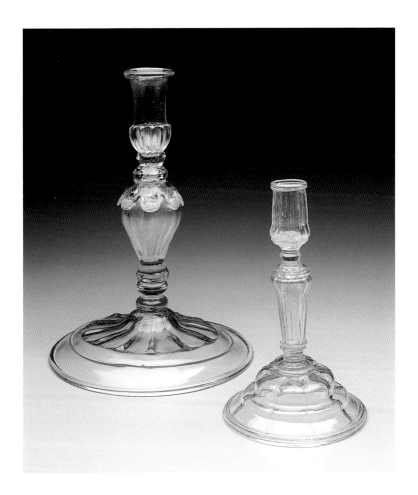

TWO CANDLESTICKS
(EACH ONE OF A PAIR)

France, c. 1700–1725 (left)
Normandy, France, c. 1725–1775 (right)
Nonlead glass
H. (left) 12¼ in. (31.1 cm), DIAM. 9 in. (22.9 cm);
H. (right) 8¾ in. (22.2 cm), DIAM. 5½ in. (14 cm)
1985.R.195, 192

THE WIDE BASE and bulbous midsection
seen in the candlestick on the left are
characteristic of late 17th- and early 18th-
century examples. However, few other
identical pieces are known to the author.
At present, only three have been located,
including the pair in the Reves Collection, that feature the combination of
ribbed foot, central petal decoration,
and fluted candle socket.

In contrast, the example on the right
is part of a well-known group featuring
raised and fluted bases, ribbed midsec-
tions, and fluted sockets. Sticks of this

type are believed to have been made in
Normandy. This part of France was one
of the most important glass-producing
areas of the country. In 1605, a monopoly
on glassmaking in Normandy and on
importation of glass into the region was
given to François Garsonnet, who established a glasshouse in Rouen. Although
he was of French birth, Garsonnet, like
many of his rivals throughout France,
relied on Italian workmen to produce
glass. Craftsmen trained in Venice and
Altare were vital to the success of the
French industry well into the 18th
century.

By 1665, the monopoly on glass in
Normandy had ceased, and the Rouen
concern faced competition from outside.
Nevertheless, it continued to operate
until the early 19th century.

CRUET SET
Probably Normandy, France, c. 1775–1800
Nonlead glass
H. 8¾ in. (22.2 cm), W. 7⅛ in. (18.1 cm),
D. 4 in. (10.2 cm)
1985.R.170.a–e

THIS SET IS AN EXAMPLE of the attractive yet functional type of glass often produced by French glasshouses. This form of cruet set, consisting of a holder containing two bottles, was popular in France throughout the 18th and into the early 19th century. Although such sets were made at many glasshouses, this particular example belongs to a group believed to come from Normandy. The engraved decoration of stars and branches is in the neoclassical taste. This style first appeared in European decorative arts in the third quarter of the 18th century and was dominant in France by the 1780s.

COVERED GOBLET AND FOOTED DISH

Bohemia, c. 1730–1750
Nonlead glass
H. (goblet) 9 in. (22.9 cm), DIAM. 3¼ in.
(8.3 cm); H. (dish) 4 in. (10.2 cm), W. 4¾ in.
(12.1 cm), D. 3⅜ in. (8.6 cm)
1985.R.260.a–b, 261

BOHEMIA IS THE ONLY European glass-making region that rivaled the fame of Venice. Rich in woodlands that could fuel the industry, the region (now in the Czech Republic) has been producing glass since the Middle Ages. By the 16th and 17th centuries, Bohemian glass dominated the northern European trade. Furthermore, adjacent areas like Silesia (part of Bohemia until 1742) worked in the Bohemian idiom. Such a transfer of style and technical skill was possible because glassworkers often moved from furnace to furnace in and outside the country. As a result, much of the glass made in Germany, Austria, Russia, Scandinavia, and the Netherlands is closely related to Bohemian products.

Both these pieces reflect the importance of Bohemian glass in the 17th and 18th centuries. Because they were often elaborately decorated, covered goblets, or *Deckelpokale,* were expensive objects and were frequently given as presentation pieces. Glasshouses throughout northern Europe produced them, and Bohemia exported them across the continent. The use of a red twist in the stem and finial and the fineness of the engraved decoration are characteristic of many Bohemian examples.

Besides goblets, Bohemia produced many shell-shaped dishes. During the Renaissance, such pieces carved from rock crystal were highly prized. By the 17th and 18th centuries, glass examples were being produced to satisfy demand. The faceted stem and radiating cutting on the foot seen here are characteristic of Bohemian examples, as is the cut decoration on the shell.

GOBLET

Central Europe, possibly Russia,
c. 1740–1760
Nonlead glass
H. 8⅞ in. (22.5 cm), DIAM. 4¾ in. (12.1 cm)
1985.R.316

WITH ITS ELABORATE rococo decoration featuring baskets of flowers and a bird, this goblet is a fine example of mid-18th-century European glass. Its exact origin is difficult to determine. Although the form and general character of the engraved and cut ornament are in the Bohemian taste, the faceted stem with three bulbs relates to examples from eastern Germany, and the cutting at the base of the bowl is sometimes seen on Russian work.

COVERED DISH
Probably Bohemia, c. 1750–1800
Nonlead glass
H. 7½ in. (19.1 cm), w. 11⅝ in. (29.5 cm),
D. 8¾ in. (22.2 cm)
1985.R.322

DISHES THAT RETAIN their original covers are rare. This particularly fine example features faceted cutwork, a scalloped rim, and stars. In both shape and decoration it is in keeping with glass made in Bohemia. Because Bohemian glass was exported all over the world, it is often difficult to say with certainty that pieces found in other glass-producing areas were in reality not imported from Bohemia. For example, this covered dish relates in some ways to glass made at the royal factory of La Granja at San Ildefonso, Spain. Nevertheless, large amounts of Bohemian glass were exported to Spain, and this appears to be such a piece.

EWER
La Granja factory, San Ildefonso, Spain,
c. 1775–1825
Nonlead glass with gilding
H. 11 in. (27.9 cm), W. 5½ in. (14 cm),
D. 4½ in. (11.4 cm)
1985.R.179.a–b

GLASS HAS BEEN MADE in the Iberian Peninsula since it was part of the Roman Empire. The sizable group of Spanish glass in the Reves Collection dates to the 18th and early 19th centuries and was probably produced at the La Granja factory. In 1728, a Catalan glassworker, Ventura Sit, built a furnace near the royal palace of La Granja in San Ildefonso. Queen Isabella Farnese was so impressed by his initial production of window and mirror glass that she built Sit a factory on the palace grounds. Besides plate glass, the factory also made chandeliers and tablewares for the Crown. However, the workshop constantly operated at a loss, and around 1760 a retail outlet was opened in Madrid in an attempt to bring in revenue. Despite continued losses, the La Granja factory remained in operation into the early 19th century.

The cutting and gilt decoration on this ewer are characteristic of La Granja wares. Spanish consumers were particularly fond of painted decoration applied in gold. Most of the examples in the Reves Collection possess such decoration. Besides its ornament, this vessel is interesting for its shape. Tall ewers with elongated spouts were first used in Asia and found great favor in India and the Islamic world. Given Spain's Islamic heritage, it is not surprising that the form was produced in glass for serving wine and other cool liquids.

WINE SET

La Granja factory, San Ildefonso, Spain,
c. 1750–1800
Nonlead glass with gilding
H. (decanter) 7¾ in. (19.7 cm), DIAM. 3 in.
(7.6 cm); H. (tray) 1¼ in. (3.2 cm), DIAM. 9⅞ in.
(25.1 cm); H. (glasses) 3⅞ in. (9.8 cm),
DIAM. 1⅞ in. (4.8 cm)
1985.R.299–301.1–6

WINE SETS THAT SURVIVE with their
original glasses, decanter, and tray are
rare. This set is also noteworthy because
of its elaborate use of painted gilt decoration in the Spanish taste. The tray is
further ornamented with a scalloped and
lobed rim. To create this complicated
shape, the hot glass was blown into a
metal or wooden mold.

DECANTER WITH TAZZA
Probably La Granja factory, San Ildefonso,
Spain, c. 1750–1800
Nonlead glass
H. 9 in. (22.9 cm), DIAM. 9¾ in. (24.8 cm)
1985.R.197.a–c

ALTHOUGH IT WAS PROBABLY produced by various European glasshouses, this form is extremely rare today. Most examples were destroyed long ago because of the difficulty of removing the decanter from the central well of the stand without dropping the top or knocking off the glasses that would have sat on the tazza.

The engraving features pomegranates, flowers, garlands, branches, and a bird. It was done by holding the glass against a rotating copper wheel fed with an abrasive. The bold yet naive quality of the engraving is typical of much Spanish glass of this period.

SWEETMEAT GLASS
England, c. 1740–1760
Lead glass
H. 6⅜ in. (16.2 cm), DIAM. 3⅞ in. (9.8 cm)
1985.R.275

IN THE FIELD OF GLASS, England is best known for the introduction of lead glass. Lead oxide was first added to molten glass at the furnace of George Ravenscroft in 1674. Through experimentation, Ravenscroft and his workers perfected lead glass in the late 17th century, producing objects that were characteristically heavy in weight and had great brilliance. By the early 18th century, glasshouses throughout England were making lead glass.

This sweetmeat glass is one of many in the Reves Collection. It is particularly noteworthy for its looped rim. Glasses having this type of applied decoration are rare. The rippled foot and the faceted stem are seen on numerous examples of fine English glass from the mid-18th century.

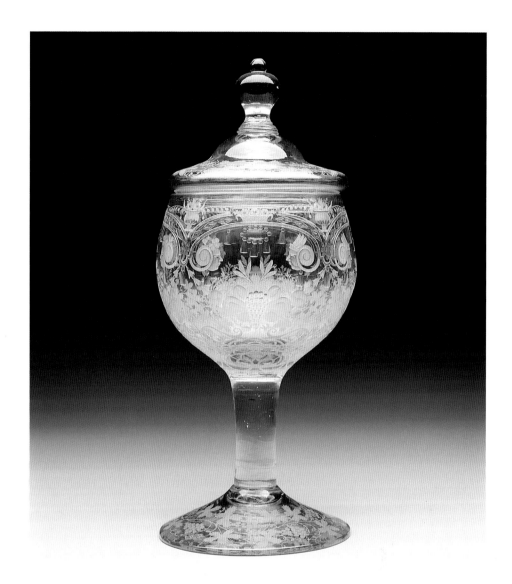

COVERED GOBLET
England, c. 1740–1760
Lead glass
H. 12½ in. (31.8 cm), DIAM. 5½ in. (14 cm)
1985.R.257.a–b

THIS GOBLET IS PART of a puzzling group of three believed to have been made in the mid-18th century (Sheppard 1990, 54–55). All three have plain stems, rounded bowls, and elaborate engraving. The other two are decorated with images of Bacchus and feature a series of musicians along their sides. Like the related goblets, the Reves one has grape vines around its foot, shell motifs at the base of the bowl, and baskets of fruit and flowers at the top of the reserves. However, the masks, garlands of fruit, tassels, and scrollwork are found only on the Reves goblet. While the decoration was almost certainly executed in England, it is likely that the engraver was from the continent, perhaps Bohemia. Numerous foreign engravers worked in England in the 18th century.

CANDLESTICK (ONE OF A PAIR)
England, c. 1740–1760
Lead glass
H. 10⅜ in. (26.4 cm), DIAM. 5¼ in. (13.3 cm)
1985.R.206

THIS CANDLESTICK and its mate take full advantage of the brilliant, reflective quality of lead glass. The rings, the ribs on the domed foot, the faceted aspect of the stems, and the balls containing air bubbles were all designed to catch the light. When holding a burning candle in the dim interiors of the 18th century, this piece of glass must have glistened beauti-fully. If desired, cut decoration could also be applied to this model. For example, the bases on a pair at the Corning Museum of Glass, Corning, New York, are cut with scallops and facets (Klein 1984, 144). Occasionally, such cut decoration was added to bases at a later date to disguise chips around the foot rim.

MUG

England, c. 1750–1775
Lead glass
H. 4⅝ in. (11.7 cm), W. 4⅛ in. (10.5 cm),
D. 2¾ in. (7 cm)
1985.R.308

USING FINE RIBBONS of glass on the lip and flutes around the waist is characteristic of English mugs made in the last half of the 18th century. This particular example is noteworthy because it is engraved with the initials *IM* and contains a Royal Maundy souvenir coin. The distribution of the Royal Maundy occurs annually on Maundy Thursday, normally in Westminster Abbey in even-numbered years, and elsewhere in odd-numbered years. Bags of money are given to as many poor men and women as there are years in the sovereign's age.

The coin in the base of this mug is dated 1687. Contemporary as well as old Maundy coins were inserted into glass objects and sold to the public as souvenirs of the celebration.

Chinese Export Porcelain

Chinese export porcelain was a particular interest of Wendy Reves's. While Emery Reves was supportive of his wife's efforts, it was she who built this part of their collection. The inspiration to collect porcelain came from the New York philanthropist Mary Lasker. Emery Reves knew her husband, Albert Lasker, through their mutual involvement in postwar humanitarian projects on behalf of displaced Jewish refugees, and the couples often saw each other in New York and Europe. In fact, Mary Lasker was the first prominent guest to stay at Villa La Pausa following its restoration. While there, Lasker encouraged Wendy Reves to begin a collection of decorative arts. Subsequently, Lasker sent her a Chinese export platter to express appreciation for a wonderful stay on the Riviera. Reves was so taken with the object that she began studying Chinese export porcelain and acquired a significant library on the subject. While traveling, she became acquainted with many of the foremost collections and dealers in the field. During the 1960s and 1970s, Reves acquired important examples in both the United States and Europe. Dealers from whom she bought include Helen Glatz in London, the Jade Company in Geneva, and A. Aronson and Stodel in Amsterdam. The *famille noire* garniture was purchased at auction in London from Christie's in 1970.

BOWL

Jingdezhen, China, c. 1640–1650
Porcelain
H. 6½ in. (16.5 cm), DIAM. 14⅝ in. (37.1 cm)
1985.R.953

CHINESE POTTERS were producing porcelain vessels centuries before their European counterparts. By the late 16th century, the Portuguese were trading with the Chinese for exotic luxuries like porcelain. The demand for this highly refined, hard, translucent ceramic was so great in Asia, Europe, and New Spain that hundreds of kilns and countless potters and decorators were employed in the city of Jingdezhen in central eastern China making wares for export. Potential profits from dealing in Asian luxury goods were thought to be so great that several European nations eventually established monopolistic merchant companies to control this commerce. The Dutch East India Company, which was founded in 1602, became the main purveyor of porcelain to Europe after 1620, the year the Dutch took over Formosa (now Taiwan). The Dutch imported blue and white ware of the kind seen here in such large quantities that it is now known as *Kraak* porcelain, after the type of ship in which it was transported.

The underglaze blue decoration on this bowl dates it to the 1640s. A potted peony bush symbolizing spring, love, and feminine beauty is depicted on the interior's bottom. On the inner wall are six panels containing stylized peach branches. The peach is believed to ward off evil and represents springtime, marriage, and immortality. The six exterior panels contain scenes featuring bamboo, flowers, and birds.

DISH

Jingdezhen, China, c. 1660–1675
Enameled porcelain
H. 2⅝ in. (6.7 cm), DIAM. 13⅜ in. (34 cm)
1985.R.858

FOLLOWING THE FALL of the Ming dynasty, during which porcelain decorated in underglaze blue dominated, Chinese potters introduced a wide range of overglaze enamel colors, producing beautiful polychrome wares. Such ware is called Kangxi porcelain since it was for the most part made during that emperor's reign (1662–1722). Evidently, little of this new multicolored pottery was sent abroad during the first part of the new reign. In 1662, the Chinese retook the trading center of Formosa from the Dutch, making it more difficult for Europeans to trade. Furthermore, the kilns at Jingdezhen were destroyed by internal violence in 1673 and not rebuilt until 1682. However, once production was revived, large quantities of Kangxi porcelain were exported to Europe, the Middle East, and the Americas.

This dish and another closely related example also in the Reves Collection have a double foot rim that Margaret Medley has demonstrated was in use between the late 1650s and the early 1670s (Butler 1990, 17 and 102).

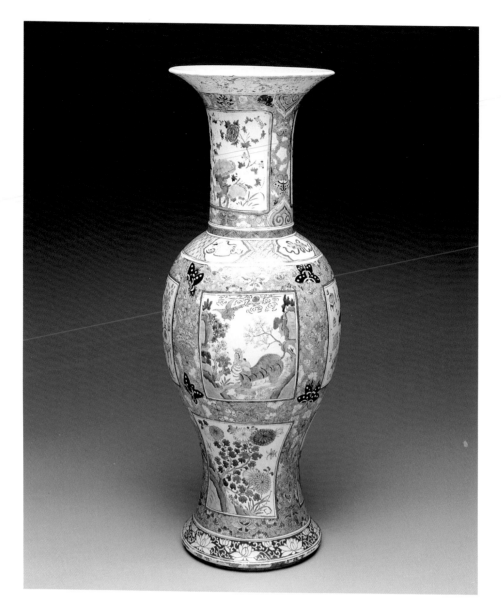

VASE

Jingdezhen, China, c. 1700
Enameled porcelain
H. 28⅜ in. (72 cm), DIAM. 10⅞ in. (27.6 cm)
1985.R.1089

IN 1683, Cang Yingxuan became head of the Imperial Factory at Jingdezhen. Under his leadership, exceptional enameled pieces like this vase were produced. Those decorated with a predominantly green palette are called *famille verte*. The Chinese called such pieces *yingcai*, which means "hard colors."

This example is a tour de force of enameling and is ornamented with numerous important symbols. Around the center section are the mythical flying unicorn and a tiger gazing at a phoenix. The phoenix represents summer and the harvest. The Buddhist "Hundred Antiques" appear in between the animal panels. On the vessel's shoulders are four reserves depicting the "Four Gentlemanly Pursuits" of music, painting, chess, and learning. The bottom has an underglaze blue double ring mark.

CHARGER
Jingdezhen, China, c. 1700–1720
Enameled porcelain
H. 4 in. (10.2 cm), DIAM. 24⅛ in. (61.3 cm)
1985.R.1060

THIS LARGE PLATE is part of a group depicting scenes from the Manchu court. Beneath flying flags, musicians play a trumpet and drum in the foreground. In the center, five warriors compete at archery on horseback as the imperial entourage looks down on the contest from a canopied balcony. Related examples illustrate military events and presentations to the emperor.

The painting on this example is exceptionally fine. The figures and architecture are well drawn and the enamels in red, blue, yellow, purple, and green are freely applied, imparting energy to the scene. The reverse is decorated with eight Buddhist symbols and scrolls supporting lotuses, as well as a double ring encircling a seal mark indicating that this plate was made as an imperial order. Apparently, therefore, the piece was exported only at a later date.

BOWL

Jingdezhen, China, c. 1700–1720
Enameled porcelain
H. 6½ in. (16.5 cm), DIAM. 13⅜ in. (34 cm)
1985.R.956

LIKE THE BLUE AND WHITE *Kraak* ware bowl discussed earlier (p. 92), this bowl is high-walled and has a lightly scalloped rim. The body is further animated by molded panels that are divided into separate reserves by the enameling on the exterior. Featured on the outside are peonies representing love, beauty, and spring; a dragon symbolizing rebirth and the emperor; and butterflies embodying the concepts of summer, joy, and conjugal happiness. The interior is painted with peony and cherry trees filled with birds.

On the bottom, an underglaze blue seal mark enclosed in a double-lined square apparently reads "made to order."

WALL FOUNTAIN

Jingdezhen, China, c. 1700–1730
Enameled porcelain
H. 16½ in. (41.9 cm), W. 8⅜ in. (21.3 cm),
D. 6⅞ in. (17.5 cm)
1985.R.843.a–b

DURING THE LATE 17th and early 18th centuries, fountains such as this, along with their accompanying oval basins, were popular among the wealthy, who washed their hands in them before meals. The depiction of sea life on this example is especially successful and well executed.

Other decorative schemes featuring birds and flowers exist on this type of fluted body, which is molded with a sinister creature whose mouth serves as a spigot.

Since the wall fountain is not a traditional Chinese form, a model must have been sent from Europe for copying. Once the Asian versions were exported to Europe, they in turn inspired copies in tin-glazed earthenware manufactured at factories in cities such as Strasbourg, France (Hüseler 1957, vol. 2, 236).

GARNITURE
Jingdezhen, China, c. 1700–1725
Enameled porcelain
H. (covered jars) 15½ in. (39.4 cm), DIAM. 9½ in.
(24.1 cm); H. (beaker vases) 15½ in. (39.4 cm),
DIAM. 7¾ in. (19.7 cm)
1985.R.957–961

SETS OF VASES called garnitures were assembled from the numerous single pieces imported into Europe for use on mantelpieces, furniture, and the tops of doorways. The arrangement of covered jars separated by beaker-form vases, as here, was typical. However, surviving garnitures with black enameled grounds, called *famille noire*, are extremely rare. The Reves example is one of only three sets known (du Boulay 1989, 19–20).

As on the others, the painting of the flowers and birds is extremely fine and executed in the typical green palette of Kangxi-period porcelains. The black enamel, which is much thicker and less well applied, was added last.

The bottom of each vase is marked with a single artemisia leaf encircled by a double ring. The artemisia is a symbol of good fortune. One lid is a replacement.

EWER AND BASIN
Jingdezhen, China, probably
c. 1720–1730, possibly 1760–1765
Enameled porcelain
H. (ewer) 12 in. (30.5 cm), W. 9¾ in. (24.8 cm), D. 4⅛ in.
(10.5 cm); H. (basin) 6 in. (15.2 cm), W. 14⅝ in. (37.1 cm),
D. 11¾ in. (29.8 cm)
1985.R.910–911

OF ALL THE SHAPES commissioned by Europeans, this is one of the most successful. A continental silver or pewter model of this form was probably sent to China for copying to ensure accuracy in filling orders. Appropriate to a vessel intended to pour water, the ewer is shaped like a nautilus and the basin like a scallop shell.

Scholars disagree as to the date of such pieces. The baroque quality of the forms and the survival of related examples decorated with *famille rose* colors suggest an early 18th-century origin. However, documents of the Dutch East India Company note that ewers and basins were first ordered in 1762 and that those requested were shell-shaped. The decoration was to be "in the Dresden manner" (Jörg 1982, 174). It is arguable that the tracery seen here is based on gilt scrollwork used at the Meissen factory in Germany during the third quarter of the 18th century. Perhaps future research will resolve this quandary.

CHARGER

Jingdezhen, China, c. 1720–1725
Enameled porcelain
H. 3 in. (7.6 cm), DIAM. 19 in. (48.3 cm)
1985.R.862

THIS LARGE CHARGER is from a series of decorative plates featuring the names and coats of arms of various cities, provinces, and countries. The twenty-three currently known are Amsterdam, Antwerp, Artois, Brabant, England, Flanders, France, Friesland, Gelderland, Groningen, Hainaut, Holland, Limburg, Louvain, Luxembourg, Mechlin, Namur, Overijssel, Rotterdam, Utrecht, Vlaardingen, Zeeland, and Zutphen. It has been convincingly suggested that such pieces were first ordered by the Dutch after the Treaty of Utrecht, which ended the War of the Spanish Succession in 1713, and were perhaps made to commemorate the Triple Alliance that linked France, England, and the Netherlands in 1717 (Howard 1978, vol. 1, 118).

The Reves example is datable to the 1720s because it employs touches of rose-colored enamel called *famille rose,* which was introduced on Chinese porcelain at this time. The underglaze blue diapered rim and well borders are also noteworthy and are found only on the series of plates in which the coat of arms is surrounded by an architectural framework, as here. The region of Namur, commemorated by this example, was part of the Spanish Netherlands during the 16th and much of the 17th centuries. Contested for by the French and English in the late 17th and early 18th centuries, Namur is now one of the provinces of Belgium.

THE PARASOL LADIES PATTERN PLATE
(ONE OF TWELVE)

Cornelis Pronk, designer; Jingdezhen, China,
c. 1736–1738
Enameled porcelain
H. 1 in. (2.5 cm), DIAM. 9⅛ in. (23.2 cm)
1985.R.1077.1

IN 1734, the Dutch East India Company
hired the Amsterdam drawing master
Cornelis Pronk (1691–1759) to create
porcelain designs to be copied in China.
Using for inspiration the motif of a
woman with a parasol that sometimes
appears on earlier blue and white porcelain, such as on a pair of cups and
saucers in the Reves Collection, Pronk
designed *The Parasol Ladies* pattern.
The designs were sent to China in 1734

via Batavia (now Jakarta, Indonesia), and
wares in the pattern were returned between 1736 and 1738 on dinner, tea, and
coffee sets. Several color schemes exist,
including underglaze blue, *famille rose,*
and the iron red seen here.

Because this pattern was extremely
popular, more examples in iron red were
ordered in the 1770s, and they vary only
slightly from the originals. Other versions were produced in Japan in the
1730s or 1740s and by some European
porcelain factories in the 18th and 19th
centuries.

The back of the Reves plate is decorated with various insects in underglaze
blue along its rim.

ARBOR PATTERN CHARGER, PITCHER
(ONE OF A PAIR), AND PAIR OF SALT CELLARS
Attributed to Cornelis Pronk, designer; Jingdezhen, China,
c. 1738–1740
Enameled porcelain
H. (charger) 1¾ in. (4.4 cm), DIAM. 14⅛ in. (35.9 cm);
H. (pitcher) 9¾ in. (24.8 cm), W. 7⅞ in. (20 cm), D. 6¾ in. (17.1 cm);
H. (salt cellars) 1½ in. (3.8 cm), W. 3 in. (7.6 cm), D. 2⅜ in. (6 cm)
1985.R.847, 886.1–2, 912.1

BECAUSE OF ITS STRONG Western composition and coloring, the so-called *Arbor* pattern has been attributed to Cornelis Pronk even though no specific drawings survive for it, unlike for *The Parasol Ladies* pattern of the preceding example. However, there exists a watercolor by Pronk of a tea pavilion in a Haarlem park dating from around 1730, and it is possible that the artist adapted this earlier effort for the porcelain. This design was apparently the fourth made especially for the Dutch East India Company. It was finished in 1737 and delivered to China two years later (Jörg 1989, 150).

These examples were originally part of a dinner service. In 1740, six sets consisting of 371 pieces were sent to the Netherlands. Three services were in underglaze blue, and the others were enameled, as here.

CHARGER (ONE OF A PAIR)
Jingdezhen, China, c. 1720
Enameled porcelain
H. 1¾ in. (4.4 cm), DIAM. 15⅜ in. (39.1 cm)
1985.R.851

THIS LARGE DISH was part of a service made around 1720 for Thomas Pitt (d. 1729). In 1717, Pitt married Lady Frances Ridgeway, daughter of the Earl of Londonderry. Following his father-in-law's death, Pitt himself was made Baron Londonderry, and in 1726 he was advanced to the new Earldom of Londonderry and constituted Captain General of the Leeward Islands in the West Indies (Howard 1974, 184).

The coat of arms are those of Pitt with Ridgeway. The motto is *Amitié* (Friendship). The Pitt set was one of the earliest armorial services ever ordered by Europeans from China. This piece bears on its reverse a *ling zhi* (sacred fungus) mark, the use of which was forbidden after 1723. At this early date, the arms typically cover the entire bottom of a dish, as here. Later, they became smaller in scale.

PLATE
Jingdezhen, China, c. 1745
Enameled porcelain
H. 1⅝ in. (4.1 cm), DIAM. 13⅜ in. (34 cm)
1985.R.1028

THE ARMS ON THIS PLATE are those of the Pigot family. The service was made for George Pigot (1719–1777) of Patshull, Staffordshire, England, who was governor of Fort Saint George in Madras, India, between 1755 and 1765 and again from 1775 to 1777. Pigot was a member of Parliament and was made a baronet in 1764. In 1766, he was made Baron Pigot of Patshull, County Dublin. He died in India (Howard 1974, 251).

The border of this example is especially interesting. At top center, it features a pelican feeding her young with her own blood, known as "Pelican in Her Piety." The rest of the design is of a trellis and leaf pattern popular on European porcelain in the mid-18th century. This particular version appears to have been copied from wares made at the Du Paquier factory in Vienna, Austria.

CHARGER

Jingdezhen, China, c. 1740–1750
Enameled porcelain
H. 1⅞ in. (4.8 cm), DIAM. 15¼ in. (38.7 cm)
1985.R.853

THIS LARGE PLATE DEPICTS the harbor of a great fortified city. Despite the presence of some European-style architecture and figures at front left, the view is probably meant to represent an Islamic trading center with its many domes and minarets. The trade theme is further emphasized by the four reserves on the plate's rim, each of which depicts figures in discussion on a riverbank outside the city walls. For both Europeans and Chinese, the Near East was an important trading partner. For example, much Chinese export porcelain was sold there.

At present, no other plate like this one has been located, although the scrollwork used here between and around the scenes is known on other pieces. Such details were initially used at the Meissen factory in Germany during the 1730s. When Europeans sent this porcelain to Asia for copying, the Chinese adapted the scrollwork and incorporated it into many of their mid-18th-century pieces.

PLATE

Jingdezhen, China, c. 1745
Enameled porcelain
H. 1½ in. (3.8 cm), DIAM. 12¾ in. (32.4 cm)
1985.R.845

THE SHELL AND SCROLL border seen
on this plate was fashionable on Chinese
export porcelain between approximately
1745 and 1755. The inner border of small
flowers is generally found through the
late 1730s. The presence of both patterns
suggests a date of around 1745.

The arms in the center are those of
the van Reverhorst family of The Hague
in the Netherlands. This plate, part of

the second of two services ordered by
the family, was most likely commissioned by Theodorus van Reverhorst
(1706–1758), who served as a member
of the Court of Justice in Batavia for the
Dutch East India Company from 1735
to 1752. The small coats of arms around
the well of the dish are those of eight
ancestral families of the van Reverhorsts.
The maternal line is on the right side,
and the paternal ancestors are on the left.
The families are van Reverhorst, Vereyck,
de Winter, de Bruyn, Shrevelius, van
Groenendijk, van Peenen, and de Vroede
(Howard 1978, vol. 2, 400–1).

TAZZA

Jingdezhen, China, c. 1752–1760
Enameled porcelain
H. 3½ in. (8.9 cm), DIAM. 11¼ in. (28.6 cm)
1985.R.870

IN THE 18TH CENTURY, Denmark traded extensively with Asia, importing numerous porcelain dinner services. Significantly, this design includes a ship at bottom center, as well as a portrait and cipher of Queen Juliana Marie, who married King Frederick V of Denmark in 1752. The central reserves are supported by the sea god Neptune and Aphrodite, who was born on the sea. These divinities, in conjunction with the ship on the lower rim and the peacock at the top, symbolize both the prowess of Denmark on the high seas and the beauty of her queen.

Although many examples from this service survive, the Reves piece is rare because of its form. Tazzas (footed dishes with upturned rims) were used on European dining tables to hold a variety of foods. This example is supported on three paw-footed legs on the knees of which are lion masks.

TUREENS-ON-STAND (SAUCE TUREEN ONE OF A PAIR)

Jingdezhen, China, c. 1760–1780
Enameled and gilt porcelain
H. (soup tureen on its stand) 8¾ in. (22.2 cm), w. 14½ in. (36.8 cm),
D. 11½ in. (29.2 cm); H. (sauce tureen on its stand) 4⅞ in. (12.4 cm),
w. 7⅝ in. (19.4 cm), D. 5⅜ in. (13.6 cm)
1985.R.877–879.a–c

THIS FORM OF OCTAGONAL tureen was fashionable during the 1760s and 1770s and was made with various finials and handles. The Reves examples feature bell-flower finials and peccary-head handles. The enameling consists of European-style flower sprigs and bamboo borders. This border design was most popular around 1770. The gilt monograms on the pieces read *PEG* and are surmounted by a crest.

It is rare for soup tureens to survive with their matching sauce tureens. The service from which the Reves examples come was probably made for the English market.

TUREEN-ON-STAND

Jingdezhen, China, c. 1750–1760

Enameled porcelain

H. (tureen) 13 in. (33 cm), w. 14¾ in. (37.5 cm),
D. 11¾ in. (29.8 cm); H. (stand) 2 in. (5.1 cm),
w. 17¼ in. (43.8 cm), D. 14 in. (35.6 cm)

1985.R.871–872

THIS AMAZINGLY SHAPED piece directly copies a European earthenware example. The form appears to have first been produced at the Strasbourg factory in eastern France around 1750. Soon thereafter, other potteries in central and northern Europe were using the form. Most notably, it was employed by the master potter Ignaz Hess while he was working at the Höchst factory in central Germany from 1746 to 1751. A tureen from one of these European sources was sent to China to be copied in porcelain. In general, Chinese potters faithfully replicated this eccentric yet bold shape. However, the decoration they applied is distinct from that on European examples. Known Chinese versions feature flowers in underglaze blue and *famille rose*. Tureens also survive that are completely undecorated, while others bear coats of arms.

On this example, the husband's arms, at left, are believed to be those of the van Dam family of Leiden in south Holland, and the wife's, on the right, are those of Count Maulde of Flanders and Hainaut.

TUREEN-ON-STAND

Jingdezhen, China, c. 1775
Enameled and gilt porcelain
H. (tureen) 9½ in. (24.1 cm), w. 14⅜ in. (36.5 cm),
D. 11½ in. (29.2 cm); H. (stand) 1¼ in. (3.2 cm),
w. 12 in. (30.5 cm), D. 16 in. (40.6 cm)
1985.R.873.a–c

THIS TUREEN-ON-STAND was modeled after a European prototype. Although the actual model sent to China could have been made of pottery, wax, wood, or pewter, the ultimate inspiration was likely a French silver tureen in the late rococo taste. During the third quarter of the 18th century, French silversmiths produced many tureens featuring elaborate finials, handles, and feet. The fluted top and sides are also suggestive of metal examples in the emerging neoclassical taste. A date of 1775 for the manufacture of this porcelain example is suggested by the fact that a tureen of the same form was part of the Royal Swedish Gripsholm

Service given in 1775 to King Gustav III by the Swedish East India Company.

Even though tureens of this model must have been expensive because of the large amount of labor required to produce porcelain of such complexity, they were popular among Europe's wealthy, and examples are known with various decorative schemes. The Reves version features neoclassical-style garlands and sprigs of flowers similar to painting found on contemporary French porcelain made at the Sevres factory. However, the masks on the scrolled handles relate more closely to earlier work done at Meissen, Germany.

TWO CANDLESTICKS
Jingdezhen, China, c. 1775–1800
Enameled and gilt porcelain
H. (left) 10¾ in. (27.3 cm), DIAM. 6⅛ in. (15.6 cm);
H. (right) 9⅜ in. (23.8 cm), DIAM. 5½ in. (14 cm)
1985.R.897, 900

CANDLESTICKS ARE UNCOMMON in Chinese export porcelain, and these examples from the Reves Collection appear to be especially rare. Both were evidently modeled after mid-18th-century European metal examples. The taller one is closely related to silver and gilt bronze candlesticks made in France and Germany between 1750 and 1775. Determin-

ing the prototype for the smaller stick is more problematic. The shape of its "drop-base" is similar to 18th-century English silver and brass examples. However, the flattened central shaft and the double ionic volutes are highly unusual and may stem from the Chinese potter's misinterpretation of or experimentation with the imported pattern.

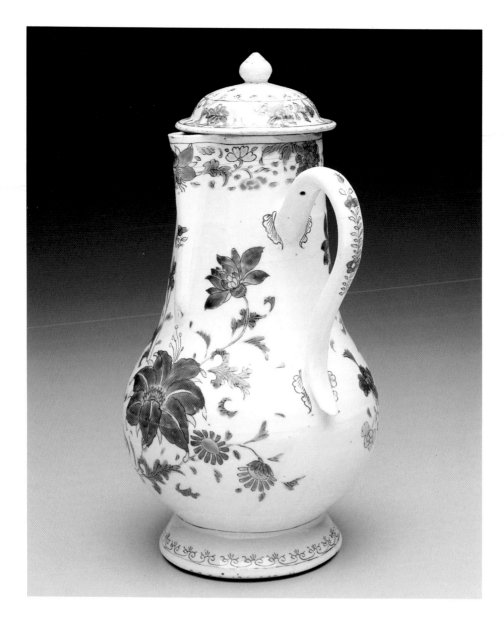

COFFEEPOT

Jingdezhen, China, c. 1740–1760
Enameled porcelain
H. 8⅜ in. (21.3 cm), W. 6¼ in. (15.9 cm),
D. 5¼ in. (13.3 cm)
1985.R.927.a–b

PORCELAIN COFFEEPOTS, like their counterparts for tea, were imported into Europe from China in large quantities. While coffeepots sometimes have handles at right angles to the spouts, as on chocolate pots, spouts such as this one are rare. Usually, Chinese export coffeepots have long tubular spouts that attach near the bottom of the vessel, as seen in European models. In contrast, the Reves pot has a V-shaped spout molded from the vessel's wall. A closely related coffeepot with a shorter but similar spout is datable to 1716, suggesting that this body form was first produced in the early 18th century (Howard 1974, 176). The *famille rose* enameling and "Meissen-derived" border on the foot rim point to a mid-18th century date for this particular example.

The lid is old, but not original to this piece.

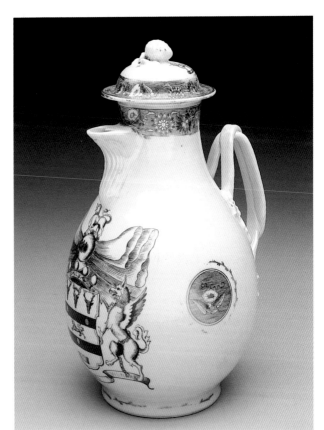

COFFEEPOT
Jingdezhen, China, c. 1790
Enameled and gilt porcelain
H. 8¼ in. (21 cm), w. 6 in. (15.2 cm),
D. 5⅛ in. (13 cm)
1985.R.928.a–b

THE BULBOUS BODY, domed lid, and strapwork handle seen here are characteristic of late 18th-century Chinese export coffeepots. The handle of intertwined strips of clay terminating in modeled sprigs of flowers was copied from pottery made in Staffordshire, England, in the 1770s and 1780s. Similarly, the linear and near monochromatic quality of the painting is derived from English transfer-printed decoration. In the early 1750s, English potters invented an ornamental process using an engraved metal plate. Once "inked" with ceramic glaze, the design was printed onto tissue paper. The paper was then affixed to the damp clay, and the printed decoration was transferred onto the vessel by burnishing. In this manner, entire sets of dinnerware could be ornamented with identical designs, thereby reducing labor costs and making ceramics more affordable. Chinese potters did not use this new process. Nevertheless, they ornamented huge services in this graphic style, painting every line by hand.

This pot features a beautifully painted but unidentified coat of arms. It incorporates a baron's coronet and the motto *LE BON TEMPS VIENDRA* (Good Times Will Come).

References

ASLIN 1962
Elizabeth Aslin. *Nineteenth Century English Furniture.* London: Faber and Faber, 1962.

AVERY 1989
Charles Avery. "Fontainebleau, Milan, or Rome? A Mannerist Bronze Lockplate and Hasp." *Studies in the History of Art* 22 (1989): 291–308. A letter from Avery to the author states that since the publication of this article other lockplates have come to light, most bearing the arms of Roman families, thus strengthening a Roman attribution (7 Jan. 1995, DMA object file no. 1985.R.814).

BENNETT 1988
Anna Gray Bennett. *Unfolding Beauty: The Art of the Fan.* New York: Thames and Hudson, 1988.

BUTLER 1990
Michael Butler, Margaret Medley, and Stephen Little. *Seventeenth-Century Chinese Porcelain from the Butler Family Collection.* Alexandria, Va.: Art Services International, 1990.

COLLINS 1988
Sheridan Pressey Collins. "The Spanish Connection." *HALI* 38 (Mar.–Apr. 1988): 42–44.

DU BOULAY 1989
Anthony du Boulay. "Kangxi—Right or Wrong." *The International Ceramics Fair and Seminar* (1989): 17–22. A letter from du Boulay to the author (22 Dec. 1994, DMA object file no. 1985.R.957) notes the existence of the third set, which appeared at auction on 27 Nov. 1990 (Sotheby's N.Y., sale no. 6105, lot 187).

ERDMANN 1960
Kurt Erdmann. Letter to Emery Reves, 28 Sept. 1960. DMA object file no. 1985.R.87.

HOWARD 1974
David Sanctuary Howard. *Chinese Armorial Porcelain.* London: Faber and Faber, 1974.

HOWARD 1978
David Howard and John Ayers. *China for the West: Chinese Porcelain and Other Decorative Arts for Export Illustrated from the Mottahedeh Collection.* 2 vols. London: Sotheby Parke Bernet, 1978.

HÜSELER 1957
Konrad Hüseler. *Deutsche Fayencen: Ein Handbuch der Fabriken Ihrer Meister und Werke.* 3 vols. Stuttgart: Anton Hiersemann, 1957.

HUTH 1971
Hans Huth. *Lacquer of the West: The History of a Craft and an Industry, 1550–1950.* Chicago: University of Chicago Press, 1971.

JÖRG 1982
C. J. A. Jörg. *Porcelain and the Dutch China Trade.* The Hague: Martinus Nijhoff, 1982.

JÖRG 1989
C. J. A. Jörg. *Chine de Commande from the Royal Museums of Art and History in Brussels: Chinese Export Porcelain.* Hong Kong: Hong Kong Museum of Art, 1989.

JOY 1977
Edward T. Joy. *English Furniture 1800–1851.* London: Sotheby Parke Bernet, 1977.

KLEIN 1984
Dan Klein and Ward Lloyd, eds. *The History of Glass.* London: Orbis, 1984.

KÜHNEL 1953
Ernst Kühnel and Louisa Bellinger. *Catalogue of Spanish Rugs, 12th Century to 19th Century*. Washington, D.C.: The Textile Museum, 1953.

PETIT 1931
Galerie Georges Petit. *Exposition de cadres français et étrangers du XVe au XXe siècle*. Paris: G. G. Petit, 1931. No. 542.

SCHEURLEER 1984
Th. H. Scheurleer. "The Philippe d'Orléans Ivory Cabinet by Pierre Gole." *Burlington Magazine* (June 1984): 333–38.

SCHEURLEER 1985
Th. H. Scheurleer. Letter to Vickie Vinson, 29 Mar. 1985. DMA object file no. 1985.R.573.a–b.

SHEPPARD 1990
Christopher Sheppard and John Smith. *A Collection of Fine Glass from the Restoration to the Regency*. London: Mallet and Sheppard and Cooper Ltd., 1990.

SYMONDS 1962
R. W. Symonds and B. B. Whineray. *Victorian Furniture*. London: Studio Editions, 1962.